Courage

# Courage and Hope

## THE STORIES OF
## TEN BAPTIST WOMEN MINISTERS

Edited by
### PAMELA R. DURSO
AND
### KEITH E. DURSO

Mercer University Press
Macon, Georgia

The Baptist Heritage & History Society
Brentwood, Tennessee

ISBN 0–86554–420-2
MUP/P320


Published by Mercer University Press
and the Baptist Heritage & History Society
© 2005 Mercer University Press
1400 Coleman Avenue
Macon, Georgia 31207

First Edition.

The paper used in this publication meets the minimum
requirements of American National Standard for Information
Sciences—Permanence of Paper for Printed Library Materials,
ANSI Z39.48-1992.

*Library of Congress Cataloging-in-Publication Data*

Courage and Hope: the stories of ten Baptist women ministers / edited by Pamela
R. Durso and Keith E. Durso. — 1st ed.
p. cm.
Includes bibliographical references and index.
ISBN 0-86554-420-4 (pbk. : alk. paper)
1. Women clergy—Biography. 2. Baptists—Biography.
I. Durso, Pamela R.  II. Durso, Keith E.
BX6493.H67 2005
286'.1'092273—dc22
[B]
2005008877

# TABLE OF CONTENTS

Preface     ix

1. Baptist Women Ministers: Called and Gifted by God     1
   Pamela R. Durso and Keith E. Durso

2. "Cherish the Dream God Has Given You":
   The Story of Addie Davis     17
   Keith E. Durso and Pamela R. Durso

3. "I Listened to the Story and I Believed"     31
   Elizabeth Smith Bellinger

4. "Yes, Lord, I'll Go"     43
   Carolyn Weatherford Crumpler

5. "The Call Does Not Stop, For New Avenues of
   Ministry Keep Opening Up"     58
   Sue Fitzgerald

6. "When God Calls People, He Calls Them to
   'Preach the Gospel' to Everyone and in All Places"     76
   Ida Mae Hays

7. "When I Am Preaching, I Know in My Bones
   that I Am Doing What I Was Born To Do"     94
   Margaret (Meg) B. Hess

8. "Let's Explore the Possibilities":
   The Story of Alma Hunt     105
   Catherine B. Allen

9. "God Does Indeed Call to Ministry Whom
   God Will, Gender Notwithstanding"     120
   Molly T. Marshall

10. "I Wouldn't Take Nothing for My Journey":
    The Story of Ella Pearson Mitchell     132
    Keith E. Durso

11. "I Am Female, But God Knew That Before
    He Called Me": The Story of Ruby Welsh Wilkins     141
    John Pierce

12. Baptist Women in the United States:
   A Selected Bibliography from 1970 to 2005          150

End Notes                                             159

*For our son and daughter, Michael and Alex*


*May you grow to be Christians of courage and hope*

# Preface

I was born into a Baptist family. Growing up as a Baptist girl in Texas during the 1960s and 1970s meant that I faithfully attended Sunday School, Training Union, Girl's Auxiliary, annual revivals, and Vacation Bible School. I memorized the books of the Bible, Old and New Testaments, as well as hundreds of Bible verses. I saved my money and gave cheerfully to missions. As I grew older I helped with Backyard Bible Schools, went on mission trips, and learned to share my faith. I also listened with enthusiasm to the stories of missionaries. I heard sermons, some very long sermons, preached by great Baptist preachers, and I sang, often off-key, under the direction of Baptist choir directors. I had a well-rounded Baptist childhood, with only one exception.

Not until I entered seminary at the age of twenty-two did I meet a Baptist woman minister. During my teen years I encountered at summer camp a Baptist woman youth director, but she was not considered to be a "real" minister, either by her church, by her youth group, or by me. One summer during my college years, I even served as a summer youth worker, but I was not recognized as a minister by the church, nor did I consider myself to be one.

In 1984, the year I enrolled in seminary, I visited and then joined University Baptist Church in Fort Worth, Texas. There I met my first female Baptist minister: Glenda Fontenot. She was the minister of young adults and senior adults. University Baptist Church recognized Glenda as a full-fledged minister. Even more startling to me was that Glenda believed that she was a minister, and she acted like one. She prayed and read scripture in worship services, and sometimes, she even preached. For the first time in my life, I began to question what I had been taught all my life: Baptist women are not ministers.

The irony of this situation is that I was a seminary student. I had been called by God. And I was a woman. Yet I was pretty sure women were not to be ministers. Glenda helped me to reevaluate my understanding of ministry and calling, and she helped me to redefine my view of my own calling. I had been called to ministry, and I was and would be a minister.

Over the past twenty years, I have continued to refine my understanding of calling and ministry, and I have had opportunities to serve in a variety of ministry positions. Among my most meaningful experiences have been my encounters with other women ministers, and I have discovered that many of them, those older and those younger, share my experience. When they were growing up, they did not have female role models. Many of them did not know a Baptist woman minister. Many of them did not hear a woman preach until they were in seminary. And many of them, like me, felt they were the only woman to struggle with calling and with being Baptist. These women shared my feelings of isolation and confusion.

In July 2004, I read with interest of the upcoming celebration at Watts Street Baptist Church in Durham, North Carolina, of the fortieth anniversary of Addie Davis's ordination. A former student of mine, Laura Johnson, served on the planning committee for that celebration. Laura is a Baptist pastor. Since 2004 she has served the Sharon Baptist Church in Smithfield, North Carolina. In the months leading up to the celebration at Watts Street, Laura shared with me her excitement about that upcoming event and her joy in meeting and connecting with other women ministers. She told me how meaningful it was to hear the stories of other Baptist women ministers. She told me of crying when she read the stories of ordained Baptist women that the planning committee had gathered. Her excitement and her need for connection with other Baptist women ministers compelled me to pursue a dream that I had held in my heart for a number of years. I knew the time had come for me to gather stories written by Baptist women ministers about their lives and their ministries. I am grateful to Laura for her role in initiating this project.

To make my dream a reality, I turned to Marc Jolley at Mercer University Press. I am greatly appreciative of his encouragement and willingness to put these stories into print. I am even more appreciative to have discovered a publisher who understands the importance of stories of faith and who has shared his own story with me.

The next step in making this dream a reality was finding women to participate in this venture. I am forever grateful to the ten women who agreed, on short notice, to write their stories or to allow their stories to be written. Libby Bellinger, Carolyn Weatherford Crumpler, Addie Davis, Sue Fitzgerald, Ida Mae Hays, Meg Hess, Alma Hunt, Molly Marshall, Ella Pearson Mitchell, and Ruby Welsh Wilkins have become my heroes, my friends, and my inspiration. I have developed a deep appreciation for their commitment to God, their faithfulness to their calling, their warmth and kindness, their humor and good spirit, and their perseverance through hard times.

The final step in the process of producing this book was to find a few gifted and willing writers. Four of the women did not have the time to write their own stories but agreed to allow someone else to write about their lives and ministries. I turned to Catherine Allen, Johnny Pierce, and my husband, Keith. Catherine has known Alma Hunt for many years, has worked closely with her, and has written numerous articles about her. I am grateful for Catherine's gracious willingness to rewrite and update Alma's story to include her more recent activities. In 2002 Johnny Pierce wrote an article about Ruby Wilkins for *Baptists Today*. That article was my first introduction to this remarkable woman, and I knew the first time I read her story that I wanted to know more about her life and her ministry in Wadley, Alabama. I am thankful that Johnny keeps his old story notes, and I am grateful for his willingness to expand and revise his original story.

I knew that I could not finish this project in fewer than six months unless I had a capable co-editor, and just as I have done for the past seventeen years, I turned to my husband, Keith, and asked him to write the stories of Addie Davis and Ella Pearson Mitchell. I also asked him edit all of the stories that I was gathering. Keith agreed, and because of his hard work, his attention to detail, and his willingness to write quickly, edit even more quickly, and proofread with lightning speed, my dream is now a reality. This book would never have been completed without his efforts, and I am thankful that over the course of our marriage, he has embraced so many of my dreams and helped me to live them out.

Included at the end of this book is a bibliography that lists selected writings about Baptist women in the United States from 1970 to 2005. In the past thirty-five years, historians and writers have produced a remarkable amount of material on the lives and work of Baptist women. While much work is still to be done, the length of this bibliography indicates the growing interest in women's history. We are indebted to Bill Sumners, Kathy Sylvest, and Taffey Hall at the Southern Baptist Historical Library and Archives, Nashville, Tennessee, for their gracious help in gathering sources and tracking down information. We are also indebted to Charles Deweese, executive director of the Baptist History and Heritage Society, Brentwood, Tennessee, for his encouragement, helpful advice, and skilled proofreading.

Pamela R. Durso

CHAPTER 1

# Baptist Women Ministers: Called and Gifted by God

PAMELA R. DURSO AND KEITH E. DURSO

For hundreds of years Baptist women have served as ministers. Many Baptists will surely consider this assertion to be overstated or even factually incorrect, and the truth is that for most of the history of the Baptist tradition, women have not held official leadership positions or titles. Baptist seminaries have been slow to embrace women as serious theological students and to train them for ministry. Baptists typically have not called women to pastor their churches. Many Baptist associations and conventions have refused to recognize women as legitimate ministers of the gospel, and Baptists, especially in the southern United States, have rarely ordained women.

Despite their lack of formal training and official recognition, women throughout Baptist history have served as church planters, exhorters and preachers, worship leaders, and spiritual counselors and advisors. During the nearly 400 years since the founding of the first Baptist church in Amsterdam, Holland, in 1608/1609, the work of these ministering Baptist women was not recorded. Baptist historians did not preserve women's experiences or record their thoughts or reflections, and few Baptist women ministers wrote their own stories. As the Baptist historian Leon McBeth observed, "Most of these historians simply ignored women. They did not say anything bad about them; they did not say anything at all about them."[1] Today, most Baptists have never even heard the names of early Baptist women leaders.

In recent Baptist life, women have had more opportunities in ministry than did their predecessors, but like Baptist women of the past, few modern-day Baptist women ministers have recorded their experiences and reflections. The pages that follow present the stories of ten Baptist women who have faithfully served and who continue to serve faithfully as ministers of the gospel. Recording the memories, reflections, and wisdom of these modern-day Baptist women ministers is crucial because they have been pioneers in the faith and have served as role models for many men and women who have followed them. Their contributions have been immense. Yet their stories also serve as a reminder of all the unrecorded stories of Baptist women ministers of the past.

In selecting a subtitle for this book, the inclusion of each word in that subtitle, "Stories of Ten Baptist Women Ministers," was intentional. The ten women who agreed to participate in this venture have shared their own stories. Most have written their stories; a few chose to have their stories written for them. These women have shared freely and honestly about their relationships with God, their callings to ministry, and their struggles with finding the right places and the right times to live out their callings. The stories of these women are still in process, for all of them are still active in ministry. These women are all Baptists and have been for decades. Most of them were born into Baptist families and have remained Baptist, and their lives and ministries have been shaped by their Baptist connections. Finally, all of the women are ministers and have been ministers for more than twenty-five years, some for more than sixty years.

In agreeing to share the stories of their lives and ministries, these ten women have participated in the long Christian tradition of preserving history and conveying truth through the telling of stories. Jesus himself was the greatest storyteller. The gospels contain many memorable parables that he shared with his listeners. They also contain Jesus' own story. The narratives of his birth, life, crucifixion, death, resurrection, and ascension comprise "a continuous story, centering upon Jesus Christ, and casting light on his identity and his significance."[2] Many of the writers of the Hebrew scriptures were also excellent storytellers. The Old Testament is "dominated by the telling and retelling of the story of how God led Israel out of Egypt into the Promised Land, and all that this implies for the people of God. There are stories of battles, love affairs, betrayals, healings, the building of temples, and disastrous sieges."[3] Eugene Peterson went so far as to proclaim, "Story is the primary way in which the revelation of God is given to us. The Holy Spirit's literary genre of choice is story."[4]

In recent years many theologians have embraced narrative theology, which pays particular attention to narratives, or stories, in relation to Christian theology. Stanley Grenz contended that this contemporary interest in narratives provides "helpful insight that points toward a more adequate understanding of theology. Narrative thinkers remind us that we must view theology in terms of its relationship to the story of God's action in history."[5] Yet long before theologians turned their attention to narrative theology and began classifying and categorizing stories according to their theological formulas, ordinary people had grasped the importance of narratives.

For thousands of years storytelling has been the means by which people introduce themselves and share their personal histories with others. Today, we continue in this tradition. We tell our stories to others and share our lives with them, but telling our stories also helps us move toward self-awareness. Telling our stories helps us define who we are, where we have been, and who we are becoming. According to Grenz, "Our sense of personal identity develops as we tell our narrative, that story in which the various threads of our lives come together in a unified, meaningful whole. The personal narrative lies at the basis of a person's sense of who he or she is."[6]

Personal stories are not our only stories. As social beings, we participate in larger ones, such as family stories, neighborhood stories, regional stories, and national stories. "Our narratives...are always embedded in the story of the community in which we participate. The community mediates to us a larger, transcending story which transmits to us our ideas of ultimate meaning."[7]

Like all other communities, the Christian community has its own story and its many stories, and as people who belong to this community, we are invited to learn the stories of Adam and Eve, Abraham and Sarah, David and Bathsheba, Mary and Joseph, Jesus, Peter, Priscilla and Aquilla, and Paul. Yet we are also invited to become part of the greater Christian story.[8] By entering into that story, we experience transformation. We encounter the grace of God and are changed forever. Our storytelling now is not merely the recitation of personal narratives but a reflection of who we are becoming in Christ. Our stories now are blended with those of other individuals and communities who have also encountered the living God, and as we begin to share our stories with others, we discover an effective means by which to communicate how God has been at work in our lives and in the world. Through this simple act of recounting our faith pilgrimage, we offer witness to all who will listen.

From the earliest days, Baptists have been storytellers, sharing about the redemptive work of God in their lives, and a good many Baptist storytellers have been women. A 1641 document identified six women, all likely Baptist, who were preaching throughout England.[9] The women—Anne Hempstall, Mary Bilbrow, Joane Bauford, Susan May, Elizabeth Bancroft, and Arabella Thomas—apparently began preaching because "there was a deficiency of good men, wherefore it was but fit that virtuous women should supply their places."[10]

Another Baptist woman who frequently and loudly told the story of her Christian faith was Mrs. Attaway, a lace-maker and member of a General Baptist church in London. In the mid-1640s Thomas Edwards, a Presbyterian minister and a vehement opponent of

Baptists and other dissenters, derisively labeled Mrs. Attaway as the "mistress of all the she-preachers in Coleman Street."[11] This Baptist "she-preacher" at first confined her preaching to female audiences but later opened her meetings to anyone who wanted to come, and apparently many wanted to come. Edwards reported that "there came a world of people, to the number of a thousand."[12] These crowds came despite the fact that Mrs. Attaway's prayers sometimes lasted half an hour and her sermons were often more than forty-five minutes.[13]

During these years in which "she-preachers" were busy proclaiming the gospel in England, the Baptist faith began to spread to other areas of the world. In 1639 Roger Williams founded the first Baptist church in America at Providence, Rhode Island. This church apparently had seven women who were original members.[14] While none of these women held official leadership positions or preached in this church, one of them, Catherine Scott, was instrumental in the church's founding. According to John Winthrop, governor of Massachusetts Bay, Scott played a significant role in Williams's acceptance of Baptist beliefs and the founding of Providence church.[15]

Other early Baptist women in America also instigated the formation of Baptist congregations. In Virginia, for example, two Westmoreland County women were the only Baptists in that county in 1773. Desiring to hold worship services, they sent an "urgent" request to a Baptist preacher named Henry Toler, asking him to come to their county. Toler's preaching and efforts eventually led to the organization of a Baptist church on April 29, 1786. By 1806 this church was the largest in Virginia. Although Toler's church-planting efforts have been recorded in great detail, the names of the two women who initiated the formation of the church are forever lost.[16]

In Louisa County, Virginia, the work and prayers of two Baptist women led to the formation of another Baptist church. In 1788 Mrs. John Poindexter and Mrs. Henley professed their faith in Christ and accepted Baptist teachings. Because many Virginians despised

Baptists, the women kept their new beliefs to themselves. For a while the women were content to pray and read scripture together secretly. Yet they desperately wanted to be part of a church. Mrs. Poindexter asked her husband to help them. Although initially refusing, Mr. Poindexter eventually relented and allowed the women to organize Baptist meetings on his property. His only requirement was that he be allowed to select the preacher. Soon after the Baptist meetings began Mr. Poindexter, who had adamantly opposed his wife's Baptist beliefs, converted, and on August 29, 1790, he, his wife, and Mrs. Henley were baptized. News of these baptisms spread throughout the area, and large crowds began attending the Baptist meetings. Like many other Baptist women, Mrs. Poindexter not only labored to found a church in her area, but her prayers and efforts also proved to be instrumental in her husband's conversion.[17]

Planting churches was but one area in which early Baptist women in America served; some also preached and served as exhorters in worship services. Many of these women belonged to Separate Baptist churches, which originated during the First Great Awakening of the 1730s and 1740s and were known for their evangelistic preaching, boisterous worship services, and emotional conversion experiences. The most prominent Separate Baptist woman was Martha Stearns Marshall, who often prayed and preached during worship services. Although her leadership in worship scandalized many Virginia Baptists, Martha's husband and pastor, Daniel, considered her preaching to be a perfectly acceptable way for her to exercise her spiritual gifts. The early Virginia Baptist historian Robert Semple claimed that Daniel's successful ministry in Virginia and North Carolina was largely due to Martha's "unwearied, and zealous co-operation." Semple described her as a woman "of good sense, singular piety, and surprising elocution," who on "countless instances melted a whole concourse into tears by her prayers and exhortations!"[18]

In other parts of the country, Baptist women also served in unofficial capacities as church leaders. In 1831 Sarah Hale's family moved from the Tennessee mountains to the Arkansas Territory and bought land in the Hot Springs area. In 1835 the Hales deeded some of that property for a church and then paid for the construction of a log church building. Sarah became the backbone of the church, making sure that it was open every Sunday for worship, and if no preacher was available, leading the service. She also provided business advice for the congregation and offered spiritual counsel and guidance for church members. Even in her latter years, when she could no longer attend church services, the deacons consulted her about church matters.[19]

Were these early Baptist women and others like them ministers? They certainly provided leadership for Baptist churches, supplied pastoral care for church members, and preached publicly. Yet they served in informal capacities, were never given official church positions or titles, and were never ordained. The questions that must be asked, therefore, are: What makes a person a Baptist minister? Should only an ordained Baptist be considered a minister?

Many Baptists, when they hear the word "minister," immediately think of a pastor or preacher. In the nineteenth century, Baptist pastor G. S. Bailey wrote a pamphlet titled *A Call to the Ministry*, in which he stated, "There is a divinely appointed and divinely called ministry…[to which] the Saviour called men specially to preach the Gospel."[20] In a 1958 article titled "Minister" for the *Encyclopedia of Southern Baptists*, Dotson M. Nelson Jr. focused solely on the Southern Baptist preacher, and in the concluding sentence, he proclaimed, "The Southern Baptist preacher—called of God, depending on the Holy Spirit, seeking always new light, ever an evangelist, continually a promoter of the program—is sometimes frustrated by the size of his task, yet generally is determined to do it to the best of his ability."[21] Bailey's pamphlet reflected the understanding held by most Baptists in the United States during the nineteenth century that the minister was a preacher. Nelson's statement confirmed that this understanding continued to be held in the mid-twentieth century.

Throughout the first 300 years of Baptist existence in the United States, the great majority of Baptist churches had only a preacher on their staffs. In the nineteenth-century, large, urban churches began hiring associate pastors or other staff members. Interestingly, some of those churches hired women and assigned them the title "Bible women" or "local missionary." These women were responsible for visiting non-members, reporting on the material needs of people, supervising mission Sunday Schools, and counseling women.[22] First Baptist Church of Dallas, Texas, had "Bible women" on its church staff from at least 1887 until 1906. While the church paid these women, they were not considered to be ministers, nor were they ordained.[23] With few exceptions, Baptist churches continued to use the title minister and to confer ordination solely on male pastors.

During the twentieth century, the definition of minister within the larger Christian community in the United States gradually evolved to include more than just the pastoral office. In 1956 H. Richard Niebuhr and Daniel D. Williams edited a collection of essays, *The Ministry in Historical Perspectives*, in which they commented on the shift that was then occurring with regard to the understanding of ministry and ministers. They asserted, "There is the astonishing adaptability and variety of the ministerial office along with the maintenance of its unity of purpose and dedication. The very word 'minister' poses the problem of the variety while it affirms the underlying unity."[24] Niebuhr and Williams then noted that to the traditional definition of minister must be added these "ministerial functions: teacher, chaplain, missionary, evangelist, counselor, and in our day of complex church organizations, secretaries, directors of councils of churches, social action commissions, and countless others. The plethora of offices exhibits the capacity of the church to adjust to new demands, and yet to hold to the core universal loyalty and function implied in all ministry."[25]

What Niebuhr and Williams observed as happening within American churches in general was also true within Baptist churches. Beginning sometime around mid-century many Baptist churches began to hire staff members to lead and plan their music programs; to work with preschoolers, children, teenagers, college students, and senior adults; and to oversee administration, education, and recreational activities. In a 1988 article, Bill Stancil attributed this growing use of multiple ministers by Baptists to the growing size and affluence of Baptist churches.[26]

Over time some Baptist churches began to recognize and to identify publicly these staff members as ministers. With these new position titles sometimes came ordination. McBeth noted in 1979 that there had been a "recent proliferation of ordination for the nonpreaching ministry."[27] For example, by 1986 a survey of 326 ministers of education in large Baptist churches revealed that 77 percent of them were ordained.[28] This changing attitude toward ministers and ministry among Baptists during the last thirty years of the twentieth century also resulted in numerous women being given the title of minister, and some of these women were even ordained.

Baptist churches that ordained non-preaching staff members often defended this practice by pointing out that God calls and gifts persons for more than simply preaching. Another reason for ordaining staff members, although often not verbalized by either churches or ministers, had to do with the practical and financial benefits that accompany ordination. In the United States ordained clergy receive certain privileges, including tax breaks and exemption from military service. According to Morris Ashcraft, if Baptists allow such privileges to determine their understanding of ministry, "the laws of the secular state, and not the teaching of Scripture or the nature of the church" are shaping their concept of ministry.[29] Given this possibility, Baptist churches would be well served to reflect on their motivations for ordaining anyone to any ministerial position and to reexamine scripture passages relating to ministerial offices and the practice of ordination. This turning to the Bible in a search for truth and guidance is one point to which most Baptists would agree.[30]

Perhaps another point on which most Baptists agree is that, generally speaking, every Christian is "minister." As Frank Stagg observed, each Christian "is a minister in the sense that each is called to a life of service,"[31] or a life of *diakonia. Diakonia* is the Greek word for "ministry" and the word from which we derive the term "deacon." This word is used numerous times in the New Testament and "whether in Greek or English, means simply 'service.'" *Diakonia* within the early church "soon came to stand for a particular ecclesiastical office, the office of the deacon," yet "its original more inclusive sense was never completely lost."[32]

Baptists have called this general call to ministry "the priesthood of believers." God calls all Christians "to bear witness to Christ, to testify to the forgiveness they have found, to pray for one another, and to give themselves in loving service to their neighbors. This is the call to the ministry, and it's a call that comes to all Christians."[33] Thus, every Baptist is a minister in this general yet vital sense of the term.[34]

Baptists have also understood that, in addition to the general call of all Christians to be ministers, there is a more specific calling of some Christians to vocational ministry.[35] For some, this special calling is to a pastoral ministry within a local congregation, and with such a calling comes the responsibility to lead the public worship of God, to instruct the congregation in Christian truth, to care for church members and offer them encouragement and admonition, and to guide the congregation in all its corporate activities.[36] For others, God's calling is to ministry with specific age groups or to specific ministries within a local church or even to ministries outside the local church.

This specific call to vocational ministry historically has been understood by Baptist as a twofold process, involving divine and human elements. God calls the individual, and a community of faith affirms that call.[37] Baptist communities since the 1650s have affirmed this special calling by ordaining those persons who have received such a call from God.[38] Baptists generally limited ordination to those men who felt called to preach. In the last three decades of the twentieth century, however, as some Baptist churches began ordaining non-preaching staff members, they also ordained persons called to "a wide range of ministries that are not, strictly speaking, oriented to the local church."[39]

This recent shift in ordination practices by some Baptists leads to the question: What is the historic Baptist understanding of ordination? Over the years Baptists have held divergent views with regard to ordination. Many Baptists, beginning in the seventeenth century, have understood ordination to be the public and ceremonial recognition by a local church that a person has been divinely called to and gifted for a particular aspect of the Christian ministry. In the 1940s the faculties of three Southern Baptist seminaries produced a booklet titled *The Ordination of Baptist Ministers*. These Baptist educators first asserted that Baptists "have historically insisted on a procedure of ordination or setting apart of those who have thus felt called in a way that recognized the validity of that call and at the same time that indicates its confirmation by the local church." These educators also noted that ordination "carries with it no sacramental meaning or authority whatever."[40] In 2003 Fisher Humphreys also advocated this understanding of ordination, insisting that "ordination is not a conferral of authority over others, but rather a confirmation and a blessing."[41]

Other Baptists have believed that ordination is unnecessary as well as not biblical. These Baptists have pointed to Baptist teachings on the priesthood of all believers and the autonomy of the local church, and they have asserted that any person, ordained or not, can perform any church function so long as the congregation authorizes that person to do so.[42] Such church polity, they have argued, means that ordination is not essential for the functioning of the church. Other Baptists have opposed ordination because it denied congregational authority. The prominent nineteenth-century English Baptist preacher Charles Spurgeon abhorred the ordination of ministers.[43] He believed that the practice of gathering a council of area pastors to examine and commission an ordination candidate allowed outside ministers to influence the practices of a local church.

Spurgeon also noted that churches in fact do not have the authority
to ordain, for:

> A true minister is a creation of the God of heaven. It is no
> more in the power of the Church than it is in the power of the
> bishops to make ministers.... God alone ordains ministers; all that
> the Church can do is to recognize them. We cannot make them at
> our colleges; we cannot make them by the laying on of hands, nor
> even by the choice of the Church. God must make them; God
> must ordain them; it is only for the Church to perceive God's
> work and cheerfully to submit to his choice.[44]

Still other Baptists believe that ordination conveys authority to
the one being ordained. In 1988 Dorothy Patterson asserted that
women should not hold a church office that requires ordination.
Among the reasons given for this assertion was her belief that with
ordination comes authority. She noted that authority is "naturally
tied to the pastoral office."[45]

Ordination debates among Baptists have become even more
common during the past forty years, and the primary reason for this
increasing interest is the issue of women's ordination.[46] In 1965 the
American Baptist Convention adopted a resolution that affirmed the
equality of women and advocated their ordination. The resolution
stated: "We believe there should be no differential treatment of men
and women in the church, family, or society and that there should be
equal opportunity for full participation in the work of our God...[and
for] full participation of women in the life and work of the church
(including the pastorate) in all countries."[47]

In 1984 the Southern Baptist Convention (SBC) stated its
opposition to the ordination of women in a resolution titled "On
Ordination and the Role of Women in Ministry," which was
approved by 58 percent of those voting at the convention. Part of the
resolution stated that, although "women are held in high honor for
their unique and significant contribution to the advancement of
Christ's kingdom,...because man was first in creation, and woman
was first in the Edenic fall,...we encourage the service of women in

all aspects of church life and work other than pastoral functions and leadership roles entailing ordination."[48] In 2000 the SBC revised its confessional statement of faith, the *Baptist Faith and Message*, to contain a clear denouncement of women's ordination and service as pastors: "While both men and women are gifted for service in the church, the office of pastor is limited to men as qualified by Scripture."[49]

Other Baptist groups have also opposed women pastors. The Original Free Will Baptist denomination, which traditionally endorsed women in ministry, began to exclude women from leadership positions in the 1950s. While the denomination has not taken an official position against female pastors and women's ordination, in recent years women have rarely been offered leadership opportunities in the churches, nor have they been approved for ordination. According to David Hines, chair of the Religion Department at Mount Olive College, a Free Will Baptist school, only one of this denomination's seven conferences currently has any ordained women serving in its churches. A second conference, however, is currently restructuring its licensing process in hopes that all potential ministers, regardless of gender, will be given serious consideration.[50]

The Seventh Day Baptists have had a similar experience. Their *Manual of Procedures* states that the call of God leads both "men and women to dedicate themselves to professional ministry." [51] Yet the reality is that only two of the approximately seventy pastors serving in Seventh Day Baptist churches in the United States and Canada are women.[52]

The National Free Will Baptists also have been reluctant to allow women to serve in ordained ministry positions. According to the Free Will Baptist pastor J. Matthew Pinson, some associations have ordained women to the gospel ministry, but most associations disagree with this practice.[53] Some Landmark Baptists have been more adamant in their opposition to female pastors. Wayne Camp asserted: "When it comes to women preachers I think that any

church that has women preach in their services are at best very
irregular and unbiblical. At worst, they are plainly heretical. I believe
it is even wrong for a woman to say 'Amen' in a public worship
service. I am not alone in that position."[54]

African American Baptist groups traditionally have opposed
ordaining women as pastors. In the 1990s ministers within the
various national African American groups displayed little enthusiasm
for the ordination of women. A survey revealed that 57 percent of
Progressive National Baptist pastors and 74 percent of National
Baptist Convention, USA, Inc., pastors opposed female ordination.[55]
In 1997 the official reports of the two major African American
Baptist groups, the National Baptist Convention of America and the
National Baptist Convention, Inc., stated that no church within their
convention had a woman pastor.[56]

Baptists have cited various reasons for opposing women's
ordination, including, "The Bible does not permit it; it mirrors the
women's liberation movement; images in Scripture are
overwhelmingly male; the woman was created second and sinned
first; the woman is the glory of man and the man the glory of God;
women are biologically and emotionally unsuited to serve as pastors;
women would be source of sexual temptation to males; being a
professional pastor would interfere with woman's roles as wife and
mother; and the church would become too feminized."[57] The most
often cited justification for opposing female ordination is that the
Bible teaches that women should not be ordained. The New
Testament, however, does not offer a clear-cut doctrinal statement
about what ordination is or who is to be ordained.[58] As the faculties
of three Southern Baptist seminaries declared in their 1940s booklet
on ordination, "There is surprisingly little said in the New
Testament about ordination."[59] The New Testament also says little
about the role of women as leaders in the church. Yet opponents and
proponents for women in ministry continue to offer proof texts for
their positions on the issue.[60]

With so many Baptist groups opposing female ministers and women's ordination and with such a long list of reasons justifying that opposition, it is surprising that in the past thirty years so many Baptist women have answered God's call to ministry, have sought church ministry positions, and have been ordained. Given the uphill battle Baptist women have faced and continue to face, one wonders why so many of them have remained within the Baptist fold. In truth, other denominations have benefited from the Baptist opposition to female ministers, for scores of women fled their childhood denomination and moved into Methodist, Presbyterian, Disciples of Christ, and United Church of Christ circles. A non-Baptist woman, Patricia Gundry, summed up the frustration that many Baptist women have experienced: "We have all too easily beaten ourselves bloody knocking at the closed doors of the institutional Church asking to be allowed into the established avenues of ministry, thinking all the while that this is the way to do it."[61]

Yet many Baptist women who have been called to and gifted for ministry have remained in the Baptist fold, and their steadfastness has brought renewal and change to the churches to which they belong. They have found ways to express their giftedness. They have found the words of Patricia Gundry to be true: "When people with ability are shut out of an established way of doing things, they tend to generate *new* ways of doing things. And those ways frequently turn out to be better—not because the people generating them are necessarily superior in ability, but because, over time, institutional structures decay. New ways can sidestep red tape and the 'can't do things differently because we've always done it this way' mentality."[62]

By remaining faithful to their heritage, Baptist women ministers have opened new doors of ministry and allowed the fresh winds of the Spirit to enter into some Baptist churches and even into some Baptist denominational structures. The names and contributions of most of these women are not known by the majority of Baptists. This book is intended, in a very small way, to remedy that problem.

Following are the stories of ten such Baptist women. The first story included is that of Addie Davis. In 1964 she was the first woman to be ordained by a Southern Baptist church, and her ordination set in motion among Baptists in the South the ongoing debate about female ministers and women's ordination. Her story is followed, in alphabetical order, by the stories of Libby Bellinger, Carolyn Weatherford Crumpler, Sue Fitzgerald, Ida Mae Hays, Meg Hess, Alma Hunt, Molly Marshall, Ella Pearson Mitchell, and Ruby Welsh Wilkins.

These women live and minister in towns and cities across the United States, in Alabama, Georgia, Kansas, Massachusetts, North Carolina, Ohio, Texas, and Virginia. They come from a variety of Baptist denominations: the American Baptist Churches, USA; the Cooperative Baptist Fellowship; and the Southern Baptist Convention. They have taken many different paths in ministry. They have served as chaplains, church staff ministers, missionaries, mission organization leaders, pastors, professors, and social ministry leaders. Some of these women have served in as many as three or four of these ministry roles over the course of their lives.

At the time these stories were written, these ten Baptist women ministers ranged in age from forty-eight to ninety-five, and they all had been serving in ministry positions for more than twenty-five years. Several of them have been in ministry for more than sixty years. A most remarkable fact about the women in this group who are retirement age is that each of them has continued to maintain an active ministry. They are busy preaching the gospel and shepherding their "flocks." Some of them have found fresh, creative ministry opportunities. They remain faithful to their calling, and they continue to explore their gifts for ministry and to take advantage of new opportunities for serving God and God's people.

Of these ten women, seven have been ordained. For those who are ordained, ordination did not come easily. Several of these women waited decades for the privilege of ordination. The women who are not ordained either were never presented with the opportunity, or they chose not to allow the issue of ordination to disrupt their ministry. Whatever their ordination status, all these women have been and continue to be ministers of the gospel. They experienced a calling from God and answered that call. They were gifted for ministry by God. They have spent years faithfully proclaiming the gospel and meeting the needs of people. They have done and continue to do the work "that the world most needs to have done" and to satisfy "the world's deep hunger."[63]

Libby Bellinger, Carolyn Weatherford Crumpler, Addie Davis, Sue Fitzgerald, Ida Mae Hays, Meg Hess, Alma Hunt, Molly Marshall, Ella Pearson Mitchell, and Ruby Welsh Wilkins have lived and ministered as women of courage and hope. They faced seemingly insurmountable obstacles. Many of them encountered educational restrictions, vocational limitations, hostile work environments, and the fear and jealousy of their colleagues. Some of these women have been ridiculed and maligned. Some were told that they were not to preach. Others were asked not to preach from the pulpit.

Yet all of these Baptist ministers courageously remained faithful to God and to their callings. Because of their strength in the face of opposition and criticism and their fortitude in pressing on despite roadblocks, they have inspired many. In persevering in the face of so many obstacles, these women restored an optimistic outlook to many individuals and churches and provided assurance that the Baptist world is changing and will continue to change. The courage of these women has brought hope to Baptists who dream of a new day when churches will embrace all those whom God has called and gifted for ministry. Our desire is that the presentation of the stories of these ten Baptist women ministers will provide encouragement, inspiration, and hope for the many women whom God has called and gifted for ministry.

# CHAPTER 2

# "Cherish the Dream God Has Given You": The Story of Addie Davis

### KEITH E. DURSO AND PAMELA R. DURSO

On August 9, 1964, Watts Street Baptist Church (WSBC) in Durham, North Carolina, did something that no Southern Baptist church had ever done: it ordained a woman to the gospel ministry. In doing so, the church not only made history; it helped Addie Davis fulfill her childhood dream. Forty years after that historic day, Addie still remembered playing preacher as a young girl.[1] Because Southern Baptists had no women preachers, she kept her dream to herself for many years. That dream, however, never left her.

Addie was born in Covington, Virginia, into a family of committed Baptists. Her paternal great-great-grandfather had been an itinerant Baptist preacher in Amherst County, near Lynchburg, Virginia. He rode approximately 3,000 miles a year on horseback, preaching the gospel every chance that he had.[2] Four generations of Davises were faithful members of the Covington Baptist Church, including Addie's maternal and paternal grandparents. Her maternal grandmother had taught a Sunday School class at the church while her infant daughter, Addie's mother, sat in her lap.[3] Addie's parents were also active in this church and made sure that she and her two siblings "were always there when the church doors were open."[4]

Regular church attendance and the influence of her family led to Addie's early interest in her faith and in following God's leadership: "I was baptized between the ages of eight and nine. I have, as long as I can remember, had a very strong religious interest. As a child, I felt a call to preach, but women were not preachers, so I never expressed this openly."[5]

Although numerous factors influence a person's call to the ministry, Addie remembered one childhood incident that shaped her sense of calling. Her mother and father were close friends with their neighbors whose youngest daughter had died just before Addie was born. The grieving parents and their sixteen-year-old daughter reached out to the Davis children and showered them with affection and attention. Addie became particularly close to their neighbors' daughter, who visited the Davis home almost daily. When Addie was eight years old, this young woman died unexpectedly, and both her life and death affected Addie deeply. Addie recalled:

> I think this acquaintance with death had a lot to do with my attitudes about life and the way I viewed it. No one in our family had died and didn't for quite some time, but she was so dear to us, and the fact is that we knew, as children would say then, that she had gone to be with Jesus. Heaven always seemed closer to me, and I was never afraid of death because of this, and I think that the beauty of her life and her patience and sweetness had its influence…. She was an exceptional person, well-loved by so many people…in her brief life.[6]

Throughout her childhood and teenage years, Addie continued to be active in church, and she diligently sought to understand the calling that God had placed in her heart. She faithfully attended the Girls' Auxiliary and Young Woman's Auxiliary and for a time considered that missions might be the vocation to which God was leading her. "I have always had a very strong feeling for missions," Addie said. "In fact, I thought a lot about mission work, but I never felt I really had the stamina that it might take to go to some of the countries where I might like to have gone. But the religious intent was always in the back of my mind."[7]

In 1938 Addie enrolled at Meredith College, a Baptist women's school in Raleigh, North Carolina, where she majored in psychology and minored in speech. After graduating from Meredith in 1942, she served as education director for the 300-member First Baptist Church in Elkin, North Carolina, and then served for four years as the dean of women at Alderson-Broadus College, a Baptist school in Phillipi, West Virginia. In addition to her administrative duties at the school, Addie also occasionally taught psychology classes.

Desiring to further her education and to pursue her call, Addie applied to and was accepted by both Duke Divinity School and Yale Divinity School. Because of her father's death in 1944, however, Addie did not attend either school, choosing instead to return to Covington to help her mother manage the family's furniture store. While working at the store in the 1950s, Addie gained invaluable pastoral experience during a six-month interim pastorate at the Lone Star Baptist Church, a rural church 16 miles outside of Covington.[8]

During the years of working with her mother, Addie became critically ill with appendicitis and peritonitis. The doctors failed to diagnosis her illness correctly, which resulted in her appendix bursting during surgery.[9] During her recovery, Addie determined that "if I was permitted to live, I would do what I'd always felt in my heart I should do, which was to be a preacher."[10]

The retirement of her mother in 1960 freed Addie to pursue her dream of becoming a minister. By this time Southeastern Baptist Theological Seminary in Wake Forest, North Carolina, had begun allowing women to study for a Bachelor of Divinity degree, which is the equivalent to a current Master of Divinity degree. Addie enrolled at Southeastern, and she felt compelled to share honestly about her calling and her desire to preach with Sydnor Stealey, the seminary's president. "I had known Dr. Stealey when I was a college student. And I told him...that I expected to be a pastor, and that was my intention, the reason I wanted a degree and to study there. He never discouraged me, but we both knew that it would be very, very difficult. And a good many of my professors, of course, were supportive. And they too knew that it would be very difficult."[11]

As Addie neared graduation, she knew that she needed to be licensed to preach. In early 1963 she talked with Warren Carr, pastor of WSBC, about the possibility of the church granting her a license.

> I felt that I had a friend in Warren Carr, and I approached him about whether or not he thought his church might back me in granting a license to preach with the idea of being ordained later. He said it sort of threw him at first, but being the kind of man he is, he said yes. And he laid the groundwork very patiently and quietly in the church among the people, and I am sure in the association among fellow pastors. As a result of that, I was granted a license to preach on March 13, 1963. This was just before I graduated in May of that year. And we got snowed out two weeks before. That was a rough two weeks for me, waiting to see if I would be approved. And the church approved. It was a large business meeting, and they had been notified. It was in the business that was to come up, and I felt very good about it. As far as I know it was unanimous. If anyone was opposed, then they must not have voted because I think the vote was unanimous as far as we can tell. There were well over one hundred people in attendance.[12]

Addie also spent those months before graduation looking for a Southern Baptist church to pastor. Wanting to stay in the South, she contacted several state executives about her pastoring a church. None of the executives knew "of any church that would consider a woman," she recalled, "and the truth is that they weren't willing to recommend a woman to any church. I had the feeling that most of them were a little bit afraid to be the first to make a suggestion like this."[13] Unable to find a Southern Baptist church to pastor, Addie contacted Elizabeth Miller, a college friend from Meredith who was working for the American Baptist Convention. Miller had been pastor of First Baptist Church in Readsboro, Vermont, and that church in 1964 was without a minister. Miller recommended Addie to the Readsboro church, and after an interview the church called her as pastor. Thus, Addie, a lifelong Southern Baptist women, moved north.

As a new pastor, Addie now needed to be ordained. She first asked her home church, Covington Baptist Church, to ordain her:

> The minister who was there at the time I went to the seminary was very much opposed to women ministers. I think the people in my church would have approved because I grew up there and they knew me. I had approached them about whether or not they would grant me a license to preach…. I had a letter from the chairman of the board of deacons at…Covington Baptist Church, stating that they were afraid it would create a controversy, which no doubt it would in most quarters. But I felt…that certainly the members would have approved, and my letter [asking for ordination] was addressed to the church, but of course, it apparently went to the minister and he took it to the board of deacons. So I simply withdrew the request…. And people still ask me why I was not ordained there, and I simply say, "Well, you had your chance." I did feel within me that I should give them the opportunity because there had been four generations of my family in that church…. But I simply felt that it was better to withdraw the request, which I did, because I did not want to be the center of any controversy.[14]

She then contacted some churches in Raleigh before finally contacting the church that had licensed her, WSBC. The deacons of the church reviewed her request for ordination. She obviously made a positive impression on the church because "the whole congregation wholeheartedly backed me," she recalled. At her ordination council, the ordination committee found her to hold a conservative theology.[15]

Carr recounted his conversation with Addie about her call. He discovered her certainty that God had called her "to be a preacher." Not once, according to Carr, did Addie express a desire to be the first woman ordained by a Southern Baptist church.[16] In fact, at the time she contacted churches about ordaining her, Addie was unaware that no Southern Baptist church had ever ordained a woman minister. She just desired to fulfill the ministry to which God had called her. Addie's ordination, Carr said, "was solely due to her personal testimony," not an attempt to call attention to herself.[17]

Addie told Carr, "I have tried to be almost everything having to do with ministry," but nothing could still her restlessness of being called to the pastorate.[18] Her overwhelming sense of call also overwhelmed Carr. He could not "escape the fact that she was called! She belonged in the center pulpit, according to our tradition, to proclaim the gospel on the Lord's Day. She was called to be a preacher."[19]

Carr chose the committee to examine Addie, and all of the committee members promised to evaluate her based on her calling and confession. On the day of the examination Addie was one of two candidates for ordination. The committee voted to recommend the other candidate, a chaplain to Baptist students at Duke University, despite the young man's unorthodox belief concerning the Virgin Birth. Addie's conservative theology, however, posed no problems for the committee, but two members confessed that despite their previous assurances, they could not recommend a woman for ordination. After a heated discussion, Carr recalled, one member who supported Addie's ordination asked the two holdouts to explain their apprehension: "Brethren, you leave me confused. In the case of our first candidate, you were quite insistent that he believe that a Virgin bore the word. How is it that you are now so adamant that a virgin should not preach the word?"[20] The committee then voted unanimously to ordain the "virgin," though one member abstained.[21]

Despite the support of the Watts Street congregation and the recommendation of the ordination committee, many persons opposed Addie's ordination. Carr received nearly fifty letters criticizing him and the church. Addie was also criticized, which she expected. Yet she was surprised at receiving letters condemning her because, she said, "If I didn't agree with something, I certainly wouldn't sit down and write somebody I didn't even know my opinion on something that really wasn't any of my business, especially in the South where ordination is supposed to be within the realm of the local church."[22]

Letters came from as far away as California. A man from Richmond, Virginia, demanded, "Renounce your ordination!"[23] Another man told her to learn from her husband, an impossible demand because Addie was not married.[24] One Christian brother even called her "a child of the Devil."[25] But Addie "never bothered to answer" any of the letters. Instead, she determined to "just take it as grain of salt and keep on."[26]

Addie contended that much of the opposition to women ministers is born "of our fatherly concept of pastors and the traditional role this has played in our lives and culture. Women make up a large percentage of our congregations and could make a difference if they were convinced that women could be pastors as well as men. And we ourselves can sometimes come on too strong and thereby defeat our purpose."[27]

Another source of opposition was that many men felt threatened by women ministers. Addie said such fears were unjustified. Women, she contended, were "not challenging men.... Men ministers have told me of their opposition because it was a threat to their ego and position, or because they grew up in the traditional way believing that only men should be pastors."[28]

As a pastor in Vermont, however, Addie found the attitude toward women ministers completely different than what she had experienced in the South. One young girl in Addie's church could not fathom a man being a minister because she had only known women pastors. As the girl and her siblings were playing church, they took turns acting the part of the minister. When the girl's younger brother announced that he wanted to be the preacher, she responded incredulously, "You can't be the preacher; only women are preachers!"[29]

Addie's church at Readsboro had about 150 members. Because it was the only Protestant church in town, many non-Baptists attended

First Baptist Church. During her years at this church, Addie emphasized pastoral care, or what she called "in-depth ministry." Although many pastors and churches considered unmarried pastors to be a liability, Addie considered her singleness to be an asset:

> I spent a great deal of time with people, and of course, I could stay much longer because I didn't have a family waiting for me at home. I realized that this wouldn't be feasible for everyone. But this is one of my strengths—compassion. I have had so many people say to me, "You were there when we needed you." So I spent many long hours in hospitals with people who were having surgery, recovering from illness, and for the most part, whenever I could, I went every day, no matter how far the distance was.[30]

Her model for this compassion-based style of ministry was Jesus, who "had all the gentleness and the compassion and the sympathy, yet he was very strong and courageous and had all the qualities that we can think of that would be worthwhile."[31] Addie believed that while men can be and are compassionate, women "bring a different perspective" and a stronger sense of compassion to the pastorate.

Addie pastored the Readsboro church for eight years. During her ministry there, the Vermont State Baptist Convention named her Vermont's Pastor of the Year in 1971.[32] In the fall of 1972, she accepted a call from Second Baptist Church of East Providence, Rhode Island, a church of about 250 members.[33]

Serving in "Roger Williams's territory," Addie continued to be a pioneer. She was Rhode Island's first woman pastor. She was also the first woman to be elected to the Providence Baptist Theological Circle and the first woman to serve as the vice president of the East Providence Clergy Association.[34] Addie later served as president of the association, which consisted mostly of Catholic priests.

During her time at East Providence, Addie found that her gender did not impede her ministry. On the contrary, she maintained that men did not have any problems with coming to her for counseling and that men often sought her counsel sooner than did women. Men, she surmised, "seem to regard me as a mother figure."[35]

In 1982, after nine years at East Providence, Addie resigned her position at Second Baptist Church and returned to Virginia after the death of her mother.

> I came back ahead of retirement mostly because of my family situation. Mother died, and she wanted me to keep our home, and my brother had died before she did.... We had always been a close family. So I either had to decide to sell the home or to take care of it.... Mother...always wanted me to have a place to come too, and I am very appreciative of that. There is no place like home. And naturally, I had no property or accumulation to amount to anything being in the ministry.[36]

Upon her return Addie hoped to find a Baptist church near Covington to pastor. Instead, she was surprised by an even more conservative attitude toward women in ministry among Southern Baptists: "I had expected to be able to pick up my work and take up another church.... But I am surprised by the ultra-conservative attitude which I have found since returning."[37] Not finding a Baptist church to pastor, however, did not end Addie's ministry. In 1982 she began serving the Rich Patch Union Church, a rural ecumenical church in Alleghany County.

During her ministry, Addie provided much inspiration for women. Her advice to women who feel called to the ministry can be summed up in one word: perseverance. "Don't give up," she encouraged women, "if you have a call from God to enter the ministry."[38] In a June 1985 sermon at a Baptist Women in Ministry meeting in Dallas, Texas, Addie offered a few more words of advice and reflections on her years of ministry:

> One. You cannot afford to be bitter. I have seen those who are in both the North and South. We may suffer indignities and vocal opposition, but bitterness has a way of turning inward and hurting

the one who harbors it. It diminishes our witness and hurts our cause....

Two. Set your priorities, your aims and goals with proper assessment of your abilities and determine to be the best of whatever you are—to give credence to your calling by adequate preparation, prayer, study and continuing education. The most important factor is to know the Lord so that no one can doubt your sincerity. Sincerity alone is not enough. Our foes are sincere, but, as we believe, sincerely wrong in their interpretation of scripture and their opposition to women pastors and deacons. Baptists have always stood for soul competency and allowed for diversity of opinion while cooperating to carry out the Great Commission.

Three. We are called to preach the gospel. I have long been aware of the importance of preaching, having had some excellent preachers in my life. There is a scarcity of great preaching today because we have come to emphasize so many other things which are important but should not take away from the art of preaching....

We need to study the Word—let God speak to us;

To preach the Word—be well prepared;

To live the Word—example is important;

To be the Word—the authentic messenger of God to others.

Four. We need to encourage one another and be careful "not to kill the dreams of others." We are in this together and need all the encouragement we can give to each other.... You and I have had and have our dreams. We may have experienced some of suffering and pain in realizing them. Don't let the dream die; don't settle for less than you feel called of God to accomplish. Encourage one another, and especially those who are younger. It is worth what it takes to make this pilgrimage of faith in largely uncharted waters. In many ways, mine has been a lonely journey, but it is most rewarding and fulfilling. My dream came true!

Finally, I believe we authenticate our ministry by being who we are, the person God intended us to be. We are not carbon copies—each one is unique, redeemed and called of God to fulfill a particular ministry. BE YOURSELF!... Your gift to God and the people you serve is YOU—you're one of a kind.[39]

Addie closed this sermon with a benediction.

May God richly bless each of you as you follow your dream; and, hopefully, as God opens doors so long shut by prejudice and lack of understanding, He will continue to unfold His will for modern-day women. The frontier is limitless in the realm of God's spirit. We humans become the stumbling blocks, often holding back the free flow of God's spirit. Women have always been pioneers, so keep on dreaming and cherish the dream God has given you! YOU WILL BE DELIVERED FROM EXILE!![40]

On August 8, 2004 WSBC celebrated the fortieth anniversary of Addie's ordination to the ministry. Addie attended the worship service and preached a brief sermon titled "Four Important Words." In the sermon, she encouraged her audience to live out the four words: commitment, trust, rest, and wait. She said:

When we accepted the Lord Jesus, were baptized and joined the church, we made a *Commitment* to follow Jesus, to honor God with our lives, to keep His commandments and to serve him to the best of our ability.

He is the source of all our blessings, the one who created us and wants us to do His will, and to rely upon Him for life and all our needs.

Commitment is walking in fellowship with God, keeping our minds and hearts open to His spirit and His indwelling presence. When we fail to do this, He is there to help us try again. Each day offers a new beginning, and God loves us despite our failures....

Secondly, we are called upon to place our *Trust* in Him, knowing that whatever we need he will supply according to what is best for us. In all of life's ups and downs, God is there to share our lives and to help us, to lift us and to enable us to keep on keeping on.... Faith grows as we trust God and walk faithfully with Him. Our trust increases, and we become mature Christians, able to digest solid food, spiritual food which deepens our faith as we come to trust Him more fully....

The third word is *Rest*. Many people face life tired all the time because of insufficient rest. We were created to need rest. Sleep renews our bodies and gives us the physical strength we need each day....

Remember the words of the hymn: "Drop thy still dews of quietness,/ Till all our strivings cease;/ Take from our souls the strain and stress,/ And let our ordered lives confess/ The beauty of thy peace."

The fourth word is *Wait*. We find it hard to wait; we want instant satisfaction, instant answers to prayer. If we are sick, we want to get well fast. We want our problems solved quickly. Waiting is not one of the best characteristics.

We are told by the psalmist to "wait on the Lord; be of good courage and he will strengthen your heart." Psalm 27:14

Isaiah reminds us "those who wait on the Lord shall renew their strength, they shall mount up with wings like eagles, they shall run and not be weary, they shall walk and not faint." Isaiah 40:31

We wait to receive God's blessings. His timing is perfect although we may not understand why we have to wait. We know He is with us. He tells us to pray and to wait.[41]

In the forty years since her ordination, Addie has practiced what she preaches. She has committed her life to ministry, even when faced with difficult barriers and almost impossible obstacles. She has trusted God to provide places of service and voices of encouragement, and she has found places of rest and refreshment. And Addie has waited patiently for God to bring about the cultural and theological changes necessary for Baptists to accept women pastors.

As of January 2005 Addie continues to live in Covington, serving as a caregiver for her nephew, Luther Davis, who suffers from kidney and back problems. Luther and his sister, Beth, a medical doctor in Oregon, are Addie's only remaining relatives.[42] Addie also continues to serve the Rich Patch Union Church. As one of four part-time leaders of the congregation and the only ordained minister, she handles most of the weddings, funerals, and baptisms.[43] Addie preaches once a month, leads a monthly women's Bible study, and does "right much hospital visiting."[44] She is grateful for this small, rural, ecumenical church because, she says, "it gives me an opportunity to serve and keeps me from getting stale."[45]

Throughout her ministry, Addie has held faithfully to the dream God placed in her heart, even though dreams such as hers are often dangerous and involve risk. In her 1985 sermon at the Baptist Women in Ministry meeting, she proclaimed that "a dream born of God within one's heart should be heeded. Human forces may try to defeat us, but the strong of heart will keep trying, not willing to have that dream destroyed."[46] Addie encouraged women to "keep on dreaming and cherish the dream God has given you!"[47] In an interview the next day, she echoed that theme: "My advice is always, if you have a dream, follow it…. Mine came true. It can be done."[48]

# CHAPTER 3

# "I Listened to the Story and I Believed"

## ELIZABETH SMITH BELLINGER

My pilgrimage of faith, so far, is a tale of journeying from "Ur of the Carolinas" to "Jerusalem-on-the-Brazos," a journey that has led me from my home in North Carolina to the wilderness of Texas. Perhaps I should not call Texas a wilderness; it is a place I did not seek, but one to which I was led. The journey has given me the opportunity to experience the love and affirmation of several faith communities— communities that have allowed me to be a storyteller among the Storytellers and to bear witness to the God who is the center of all stories.

Like Charles Dickens, perhaps I should begin at the beginning. My mother was rushed to the hospital during a snowstorm the January night that I was born in 1948. The small town of Lexington, North Carolina, is the community of my birth and upbringing. A happy baby was brought into a loving and happy home. I was surrounded by a strong group of matriarchs. Three generations of women supported me with their love. My father was the tall fortress that protected my brother and me. My mother's side of the family was Methodist. My father's side was Baptist. We attended First Baptist Church of Lexington. My father's brothers were faithful deacons, and my grandmother was a scrutinizer of the pastors. However, I would not describe my family as particularly religious. We only studied our Bibles in order to mark the contribution envelopes. We certainly did not have perfect attendance, but we were there often and gave faithfully.

My earliest memory of church is a warm and sheltering one. One summer when I was a preschooler, my aunt took us to Vacation Bible School. We arrived late, and the assembly was over. The old sanctuary was dark and deserted. I remember feeling small and lost. I do not know why I was alone; I only remember standing in the aisle and seeing the skirt and legs of a woman coming toward me. She picked me up and said, "Don't worry. Everything's all right. Let's go find your teacher, and I'll show you which room you are in." I will forever love the smell of old, dark, musky churches because they feel like home to me. They feel like a place that is accepting, nurturing, and loving. When our new church building was constructed, I remember being sad that the old church was being torn down because it was such a place of safety for a small child. I grew as a person and was nurtured by a loving and caring community. The church was like a second family for me.

Being "raised right" in the Baptist tradition, I was involved in Girls' Auxiliary (GA), a training program for future members of the Woman's Missionary Union or workers for the mission fields. I remember having more passion for Young Woman's Auxiliary, the group for teens. My aunt and one of her friends led this group, which was far less dictatorial and much more inclusive than the GA group. The mission stories also seemed much more personal. I feel that these programs for girls planted the seeds that later blossomed into many women entering the ministry.

At the Baptist age of accountability, age twelve, I made the decision to join the church. Perhaps it was because some of my friends were joining, but there was something else. I was a shy child and did not like getting up in front of people, so for me to "walk the aisle," something had to move me. I remember the feeling that a presence was with me as I made my decision, and a cloak of joy and peace seemed to enfold me.

Earlier, when my older brother was baptized, my mother was baptized at the same time. When I asked her about that experience, around the time of my own baptism, she said that she was raised as a Methodist and that Methodists did not baptize by lowering someone totally under the water. My mother was terrified of water, even bath water, but she felt that she needed to be a witness to my brother. If she was encouraging him to be "dunked" in order to be a member of a Baptist church, then she too should be immersed. She made it quite clear to me that the sprinkling that she had as a child in the Methodist church was significant for her. It was "good enough." It had the same effect of announcing that she was a Christian, but if "going under" was what was required to be fully a member of the First Baptist Church, then she would do it. Her primary motivation, however, was quite clear; she wanted to be a witness for her children. She would *never* have gone into the baptismal tank otherwise.

The First Baptist Church of Lexington was a conservative place, but not fundamentalist. The "fundamentalist" church was on the other side of town. We knew which one it was, where it was, and that it should be avoided. First Baptist, Lexington, was for me a place that was nurturing and encouraging. The worship services, especially the candlelight service at Christmas, were always inspirational. The music of the church and the organist were always topnotch and were especially meaningful for me during my high school years.

One minister of education at First Baptist made a pointed effort to help us as teens decide what we believed, why we believed it, and how it contrasted with what other denominations believed. He took us on a tour of Lutheran, Presbyterian, and Moravian worship services. Looking back, I now recognize his openness was rather advanced for the late 1960s.

Later, when I was in college and seminary, First Baptist, Lexington, could be clearly described as a "moderate" Baptist community of faith. I remember attending an ecumenical worship celebration there one weekend. Gone were the revivals of old. This service had no altar calls that went on endlessly. In place of the revival, the church was now hosting a community service open to everyone. The Baptists hosted it, and the Lutheran pastor and the Catholic priest led the "liturgy." Carlyle Marney was the proclaimer, and the Moravians conducted communion so that everyone could participate together. It was most inspiring. In the mid-1970s when I returned home for the holidays, First Baptist was celebrating Advent with an Advent wreath and a Chrismon (Christ Monogram) Tree in the sanctuary. As a child I had been taught that a Christmas tree must never be in the sanctuary but only in the fellowship hall. As I had grown, so too had First Baptist Church, Lexington. It had not remained static or complacent.

Several individuals influenced me in the early years of my Christian pilgrimage. My great-grandmother was the most influential family member because she made the presence of God a reality. Through her life and in her eyes, I could see God and feel God's love. Her faith was an inspiration. She had endured many hardships, but her face could radiate peace and joy. She was my unconditional love person; she remains one of my "balcony people," my greatest supporters. My mother was also a wonderful influence. She would never claim this influence, but through her life I saw how to care for other people. I witnessed kindness, graciousness, and a mischievous sense of humor. She also taught me that one should not judge other persons without knowing their story. She specifically recounted family stories to explain the burdens that different people had and how these burdens influenced their behavior. My mother was warm, open, and receptive to everyone once she knew them.

The two most influential people in my church were my pastor and my minister of music. Both came into my life around the same time. The first funeral conducted after David Hoke Coon became our pastor was that of my Grandmother Smith. Rev. Coon was kind, considerate, and present. His preaching was thoughtful and well prepared. He was an encourager. When I was in my third year of seminary, he asked me if I had thought of ordination. I was shocked and said that I had not. Rev. Coon suggested that I think about it and said, "If you were a man, Libby, you would already be ordained or be planning it for when you receive your degree." He was a mentor and friend.

Our minister of music at First Baptist Church was a woman, Jeanne Saunders Davis. She was the first woman whom I had ever seen in a church staff position other than secretary. We did not have a youth program in those days, but we did have a youth choir. Jeanne ministered to us through the music program of the church, helped plant the seed that a Christian vocation might be my calling, and provided the insight that God needs women in the ministry.

Jeanne Saunders Davis and David Hoke Coon were each, in their own ways, mentors. Each expressed and lived what being a Christian meant. Both encouraged me to consider how God was leading my life. Jeanne particularly was a friend, confidant, and counselor.

When I entered Atlantic Christian College (now Barton College), a small Disciples of Christ school in Wilson, North Carolina, I rebelled against the urgings to follow a Christian vocation, but by my sophomore year I could not resist the feeling of being led in this direction. Following this calling, I changed my major from art to religion and began to prepare myself for seminary and Christian ministry. The religion courses that I took excited me; they were wonderful. I heard things in them that I had never heard in Sunday School. I remember that in my first religion class we read a text titled *People of the Covenant*. I had no idea that this book had raised a controversy among Baptists and that later the man I married would teach with Jack Flanders, one of the book's authors. I found *People of the Covenant* stimulating and enlightening, and I wondered what more there could be out there to learn about God and God's people. The Religion in America and Christian Social Ethics courses were also eye-opening and mind-expanding classes. I remember reading H. Richard Niebuhr's *Christ and Culture* and feeling changed forever. I read Rudolf Bultmann, who said that the thing that really bothers religious folk—what trips us up in the New Testament—is not talk about demons, angels, a heaven above, a hell below, or a Jesus who walks on water and gets raised from the dead. What trips us up is the call to "authentic existence." In these words, I found a phrase upon which I could build. I had a goal, a direction toward which I could grow as a Christian.

College also offered me the opportunity to experience more leadership roles. As president of the Baptist Student Union, I was introduced to the wider community of Baptist students at other universities in North Carolina. Those students were inspiring and motivating. I found myself in leadership roles that I would never have normally sought.

While the minister of music at my home church was the only model of a woman in ministry that I had seen, I knew I could not be a minister of music because I cannot read music. So I began the search for a ministry option that would fit with my gifts. In 1970 I went to Southeastern Baptist Theological Seminary in Wake Forest, North Carolina, with the goal of getting a two-year degree in religious education and finding a job as a youth minister. At that time, the women's dorm at Southeastern housed fifty-seven students. Thirteen of us lived on the first floor. Some of the women had been Journey*men* (mission field placements usually two years in duration) for the Southern Baptist Convention (SBC). Since I had been taught that being a missionary was the ultimate achievement, I felt small and unprepared compared to those Journeymen. Other women on my floor had already served on church staffs in educational or youth-related positions.

I was ready to pack my bags and head home until another student asked me an important question: "Libby, have you ever experienced, felt, the grace of God?" Since we were studying Paul Tillich's *Systematic Theology* at the time, I was sure that her question related to something she was reading. But she persisted and asked the question again in another way: "Libby, do you know that God loves you unconditionally?" I began to cry because I had never thought about it that way. She went on to witness to me about God's grace, love, and acceptance. I must admit that this was really the first time that I had ever experienced God's grace for myself.

I continued with my seminary work. I took two clinical pastoral education classes that were invaluable in helping me see myself as a minister. As a chaplain at Dorothea Dix Mental Hospital in Raleigh, North Carolina, and at the Baptist Hospital in Winston-Salem, North Carolina, I was given the opportunity to experience the role of minister. Both of these programs helped me to understand better the needs of people and how to minister to those needs. In these programs, my gift for listening was heightened and expanded. I came to understand that listening is a ministry in itself.

I received encouragement to be a minister at Southeastern and was redirected to the Master of Divinity program. One professor asked me if I was sure that I wanted to remain a Baptist. He saw the changes taking place in the SBC and knew it would become an inhospitable place for women educated for ministry. He also helped me find an internship in campus ministry at North Carolina State University—a wonderful ministry opportunity. I had served less than a year in this internship position when the supervising chaplain took a sabbatical leave and then quit his position. I was asked to be the interim campus minister. I served in this position for six months. I knew I had done a good job and had related well to students. I was recommended by my supervisor to be his replacement, and then I encountered a roadblock. The Baptist state convention director of student work wanted an ordained, married, male pastor with experience. Since I was not male, was not ordained, was not married, and had no experience on a church staff, I certainly did not fit his criteria for this position. I was devastated. I asked myself, "Was God actually calling me to ministry?"

During this time, I had been encouraged to consider ordination by my campus ministry supervisor, and once again my home pastor was asking me about ordination. I needed time to think about and discern God's leading.

I reenrolled at Southeastern Seminary in the Doctor of Ministry program, and as part of the reflection needed for that degree, I worked through what I was hearing as God's leading. On April 13, 1975, the First Baptist Church of Lexington, North Carolina, ordained me. It was an inspirational time. I faced little opposition in contrast to that experienced by other women seeking ordination at that time. My pastor's question was, "Why has it taken you so long to do this?"

I believe that women take the ordination issue much more seriously than do men because we have to do so. During the 1970s, Baptist women seeking ordination were being rejected, ridiculed, and told that they were not really hearing the word of the Lord. The word of the Lord was being reserved for men only.

At my ordination, a special person was involved in the service—Bill Bellinger, a young seminary student whom I had met the previous summer. He encouraged and supported my desire to be a minister. He was so supportive that in September of that same year we were married.

You may notice that I have not mentioned the desire to be a "pastor." I did not know any woman who was serving as pastor of a church at that time. I also knew that I was moving with my husband to England, where he was going to work on his doctoral degree in Old Testament studies. We spent three years in England, and there, so far away from family and friends, we established a strong partnership. I did not have a paid ministry position in England but did serve as a deacon in St. Andrew's Street Baptist Church and was involved in a ministry to their homebound elders.

My husband's career then led us to Arden Hills, Minnesota, where he taught at Bethel Theological Seminary. I worked first as an assistant to the dean of the college that was connected to the seminary; later I served as the associate pastor at Spring Lake Park Baptist Church in Spring Lake Park. Our first child, Gillian, was born shortly after I joined the church staff, and this community of faith supported us. The congregation gave me my first opportunities to preach. For a conservative, traditional group, they were very trusting and affirming. Minnesota was a place of grace for us for three years. Then, my husband received a call to teach at Southwestern Baptist Theological Seminary in Fort Worth, Texas.

Based perhaps on our three-year stay in Fort Worth, I describe Texas as a wilderness. While living in Fort Worth, I did not find employment as a minister. The seminary had plenty of students to fill staff positions, interim positions, and even supply-preaching positions. I felt much more than ever before that because I was an ordained woman minister and held a doctoral degree, I was not welcome to hold leadership roles in Baptist life. Those years were a time when I felt professionally stagnant. I was involved in the life of our community of faith and often led small groups or retreats for other communities of faith, but professionally I felt that I was wandering in the wilderness. I did manage to be fruitful and multiply. Our second child, Chip, was born in Fort Worth.

In 1984 my husband was called to the faculty of Baylor University (Jerusalem-on-the-Brazos). We figured that it would be yet another three-year rotation, but Waco has been our home for twenty years. It is a nurturing place and I have found a community that has embraced and encouraged me. I was hired as a nursing home chaplain by a social service agency that worked with the elderly. Even though I was quite comfortable around the elderly, I had never considered ministry in a nursing home setting. This position proved to be quite similar to being the pastor of a congregation. Instead of one flock, however, I had five flocks, which I tended each week. The nursing home residents demonstrated perseverance, steadfastness of spirit, grace under trying circumstances, and the power of prayer in a time of "being, not doing."

I had several unexpected opportunities for leadership after we moved to Waco. The Waco Ministerial Alliance graciously selected me as its first female vice president and president. At the ministerial alliance banquet the year I was elected vice president, a Catholic Monsignor installed the officers. He called each of us forward. He gave me a puzzled look and proceeded to introduce the other officers. The new president realized that he had overlooked me in the introductions and said, "Monsignor, this is our new vice president, Libby Bellinger." Obviously taken aback, the monsignor gave me a long look, chuckled, held out his hand, and said, "Well, I'll be darned! Where will they [women] be next?" The rabbi seated on the front row quickly answered, "In the priesthood, in the priesthood!"

During the early years in Waco, I was also elected to the Southern Baptist Women in Ministry steering committee and later became the organization's president. The Alliance of Baptists also gave me an opportunity to serve on its board during its formative years. These were days of turmoil for Baptists. The SBC was beginning to be controlled by the fundamentalists. I remember giving an interview following the establishments of the Alliance and of the Cooperative Baptist Fellowship in which I said that Southern Baptist women who follow God's call to go into the ministry face a doubly frustrating challenge. They are frustrated on the one hand by fundamentalists and on the other by moderates. The fundamentalists say women cannot be ordained, whereas the moderates vocally support us but do not hire us. I advised women who wished to be ordained to consider carefully the denomination to which they wanted to be linked.

I did not decide to join with another denomination; I am, however, no longer a "Southern" Baptist. The congregation of which I am a member made a conscious decision to break our allegiance to the SBC. Yet I do very much see myself as Baptist. I affirm distinctive Baptist principles such as the priesthood of believers and the autonomy of the local church. In 1994 Judson Press published a book that I edited titled *A Costly Obedience: Sermons by Women of Steadfast Faith*. This book features sermons preached by women at the annual Baptist Women in Ministry meetings and in various worship settings. In collecting and editing these sermons, I hoped to give a larger community the opportunity to hear the voice of Baptist women preachers.

My pilgrimage can be described rather simply and easily. Basically, the scenario goes like this: I listened to the Story, and I believed. When as a child the community of faith told me Jesus loved me and when they demonstrated that love through their lives, I believed. When I sang as a GA, "We've a Story to Tell to the Nations," I believed. When in Baptist Student Union, we sang "Be Thou My Vision," I believed. When in seminary I was shown God's grace, I believed. In word and music and example, the Story was heard and believed.

I am a product of the system in which I was raised. I listened to what it was saying and acted upon what I heard. There was only one problem that confused me—I did not realize the Story was just for men. And so I proceeded to act as though the Story was for everyone and to believe that the dreams and visions I was having were authentic and authoritative.

A group of creative conservatives affirmed those dreams and visions through the laying-on-of-hands and by sending me out to be a storyteller. I even met an individual who saw some of the same dreams and visions; and we seemed favorable in each other's sight and decided to tell the Story together. We are still doing that even though Bill tends to tell the Old Testament version of the Story.

My pilgrimage of faith is a journey that has allowed me to minister to the elders of the Waco community. After I served as a nursing home chaplain, I became the assistant director of Inner City Ministry (now Central Texas Senior Ministry), a social service agency in Waco. My twenty years of ministry in that agency have allowed me to build strong bonds in the Waco community. My twenty years of service as a member of Lake Shore Baptist Church in Waco have been empowering and enriching. Lake Shore is a congregation that strives to be truly Baptist in nature. It seeks to be responsive to the city of which it is a part. It tries to speak a word of hope to a troubled world. It is a community of faith that has focused my preaching, sharpened my teaching, and enlarged my understanding of missions and ministry. It is a church that has two women as pastors: two women serving a Baptist church in Texas, and I get to be a member! Surely, the Lord is in this place, and we are blessed.

CHAPTER 4

# "Yes, Lord, I'll Go"

## CAROLYN WEATHERFORD CRUMPLER

"Carolyn, one of these days you're gonna dig so far you will get to China!" my daddy said, as he looked down into the hole that my friends and I had dug in the back yard. He had given permission for digging the hole, but he had not realized how many playmates would be helping. Through the years, I kept digging in various ways, and finally, I did get to China.

My story is one of a girl born into a Christian family. We lived in Frostproof, Florida. Sunday School, Sunbeams, then Girls' Auxiliary (GAs), Training Union, missionary visits, and summer mission camps defined my growing-up years. During my teenage years, my unmarried, female high school teacher left teaching and went to seminary. So as far as I knew, there were no limits to what I could do. When I was fourteen years old, I was told that I would be the leader of the younger GAs. I can still see the stunned expression of the state Woman's Missionary Union (WMU) young people's secretary when she got off the bus and saw that I was the leader whom she had come to train! When I was fifteen years old, our pastor visited my parents and asked them if they would permit me to teach the younger boys in what was then called the junior department.

When I was sixteen, that same WMU state youth leader was speaking in our area, and she encouraged my mother to let me go with her and some other Florida girls to Ridgecrest, a Baptist camp in North Carolina. At Ridgecrest, I first sensed a direct call to "full-time Christian service." I met missionaries. I heard presentations by the four men who headed the four boards of the Southern Baptist Convention (SBC) and was impressed that they took time from their work to attend a conference for young women. At the end of the week, I said, "Yes, Lord. I'll go."

When I returned home and shared the news with my parents and my church, my pastor said, "You know, Carolyn, a call to serve is a call to prepare." He then began preparing me. I was assigned the task of leading a group in the association. The next year, when the state music department sent a musician to work with our choir, I learned how to "beat time" better than anybody else, and at seventeen, I became the choir director of First Baptist Church in Frostproof.

After graduating from high school, I attended Florida State University in Tallahassee. I moved my church letter to First Baptist Church, and I joined the Baptist Student Union (BSU). All my spare time was spent in these two places. I was elected missions chairman for the BSU, and my only experience with "being campused," or disciplined, was when I went to a little country church to speak, and forgot to sign out!

While in college, I found it difficult to declare a major. Everything interested me. I finally decided in my junior year to enroll in the new School of Library Science. Graduation brought another new chapter—public school teaching. I became the librarian at Eustis High School in Eustis, Florida, where I stayed for two years before moving to a larger school, Hillsborough High School in Tampa, Florida. I joined Seminole Heights Baptist Church, a large church with a strong missionary history. Four couples from that church were on the foreign mission field. A woman member was a professor in a seminary. Because I was a librarian, I did not have to grade papers or do a lot of work after hours, so I spent a lot of time at the church. Two summers I served as youth director. I was supremely happy and very busy.

In my third year in Tampa, Seminole Heights had a revival led by the late Dr. Charles Howard. He concluded one of his messages with this quote: "Lord, send me anywhere, only go with me; place any burden on me, only sustain me; sever any tie, save the tie that binds my heart to yours." His words were the ones I needed to hear. I realized that I had become so comfortable, so tied to my life as it was, that I had forgotten that I had a calling. I "walked the aisle" and announced my decision to go to seminary. My church endorsed me, and away I went to New Orleans to attend New Orleans Baptist Theological Seminary (NOBTS). The school was my choice, though I was greatly encouraged to choose another. My decision was based on my meeting and hearing Gladys Keith, a missionary in New Orleans. I wanted to go and work with her in the "wicked city of New Orleans." Many years later when I met Dr. Howard, I told him of the blessing his revival sermons had been to me. He clasped my hand and said, "Oh, thank you. I always looked back on that revival as being one of my biggest failures. Now I know that it was not. Thank you!"

Now I must insert that the year was 1956. At that time, I did not know that people serving in ministry positions other than pastor could be ordained. But when I left my church in Tampa, the one in which I had served as part-time youth director, the members decided that they needed a full-time youth director, so they, who had been my dear friends and supporters, elected a man, changed the title to youth minister, and ordained him.

In 1956 I also had never heard of a Baptist woman preacher, and I knew there were no women pastors in Southern Baptist churches, although one of my women teacher friends in Tampa was also pastor of a Methodist church. But when I enrolled at NOBTS, my innocent, feminine eyes were opened. Never before had I encountered the thought that, because I was female, there were things I would not be permitted to do. What a shock I received when I arrived on the lovely seminary campus. I was told that I could not enroll in the school of theology. Why? I was a woman! And I could not enroll in the school of music because I could not carry a tune. The only option left was the school of religious education. I breezed through those religious education courses. I had studied much of the same content in church study courses through the years. The best part of that experience was that I could take all my electives in theology, and I did. I only regret that did not take a course in homiletics because I have been sermonizing ever since then.

That the Lord had been working on me all along was evident when the dean of students, Helen Falls, told me that Harriett Mather, the directress of the Mather School of Nursing at the Baptist Hospital in New Orleans, wanted to see me. She had heard that a librarian had enrolled at the seminary, and she needed a librarian. For the two years that I was in New Orleans, I was the librarian at the nursing school, which had been founded in 1929 and had never had a trained librarian.

While at seminary, in my final year, I met with two men to discover possibilities for a position after graduation. The executive from Florida was glad to see me, for I had been a "state approved worker" and had led conferences during my school teaching years. As I talked with him about possibilities in Florida, he patted my shoulder and said, "Now, Carolyn, I suggest that you find one of these fine preacher boys, marry him, and come home to Florida to work." The male representative from the mission board assured me that it would be better if I married before seeking missionary appointment. Fortunately, I also had contact with people like Edna Frances Dawkins, who served in the personnel department of the Foreign Mission Board. Efie, as we called her, was a great advocate for and encourager of women.

In 1958, with my master's in religious education achieved, I was ready for the next step. I had interesting interviews, but my final choice was to go to Alabama as the director of the Young Woman's Auxiliary for the Alabama WMU. In my first year there, I attended a world missions conference and heard Baker James Cauthen say, "If God has not told you to stay, you might need to go." I immediately contacted the SBC's Foreign Mission Board. At about this time, I was diagnosed with high blood pressure and was told by the board to "wait and see." Soon after this diagnosis, I was invited to go to the Florida WMU as Girls' Auxiliary director, and I saw this as the perfect time to return to my home state while awaiting my health verdict. After three years in Florida, I went back to Alabama as promotion division director for the Alabama WMU, and by this time it was evident that my deep love for missions would be carried out, not overseas, but through missions organizations in churches. I was called to the stated purpose of the WMU, "to stir up the missionary zeal." After my second term with the Alabama WMU, I was called back to my home state to become the executive director of the Florida WMU, where I remained for seven years before becoming the executive director of the national WMU. For fifteen years, from 1974 to 1989, I led the national organization.

In 1964, the year Addie Davis was ordained, Southern Baptists began expressing concerns about women's rights and feminism. Young women were beginning to question the limitations that they were facing. I remember sitting at coffee break in the late 1960s with some of the women in the Florida Baptist building. I commented that I was not too concerned about the "women's rights issues"—that I did not need ordination, nor did I fear that my job would be taken by a man. One of the young women said, "But, Miss Weatherford, we are desperately concerned, and you are our leader. You have to care."

In 1974, after my election in Dallas, Texas, as the executive director of the national WMU, I was interviewed by the press. One of the first questions was, "What is your stand on the issue of women?" In an effort to stress that I was for all individuals—female and male—I blurted out, "Oh, I'm not a feminist. I'm a humanist!" That was my first major blunder before the press, but surely not my last. Later, in a warm, friendly setting with home missions personnel, someone broached the subject of job security for women. I assured the mostly male audience, "I'm not worried about my job. No man wants my job." To the laughter and clapping crowd, one man stood up and said, "Oh, Carolyn. I do. I've always wanted to be the WMU director!" But fun aside, the issue of women was a big topic throughout my days as WMU executive director. Christine Harrison Gregory was my first WMU president, and she, though married and a homemaker, stood beside me as we attempted to make women a recognized force in Baptist life.

My first major encounter over the issue of women came in 1976, in Columbia, South Carolina. The interdenominational Christian Action Council held a weekend conference on the topic of women in the church. I was invited as one of the speakers. Among the many statements I made during that weekend was a brief disparaging remark about a then popular book, *The Total Woman*. On Monday morning, I was called by a friend at *Baptist Press*. He quoted from the Columbia newspaper, and said, "Carolyn, did you really say that?" I said, "Oh yes, but let me tell you about the other things. I made a really good speech." He listened and then replied, "But, Carolyn, that is not newsworthy. This is!" So the article, "WMU Leader Smacks *Total Woman*," came out and was carried by most state Baptist papers.

We had about 130 letters about my remarks, but the overwhelming majority of the letters were favorable. But the few negative ones really hurt. I had never been hit with such a barrage of anger. I even sought counsel from my pastor. Fortunately, though, I learned that this was going to happen if I continued to speak boldly, and I knew that I was going to continue speaking boldly.

As an executive of an SBC institution, I served on the Inter-Agency Council, an agency that no longer exists. Always, in that astute group, there had been only one woman present, the WMU executive. I loved being with those men in planning sessions, in times of visioning, and in times of hard work. In 1978 that group planned a "Consultation on Women in Church-Related Vocations." Although I and one or two of the men wanted to use the term "women in ministry," we were outvoted. Nevertheless, the consultation was an excellent meeting, with the WMU staff members taking major responsibilities, and there were many good results. The WMU always regarded women missionaries as "women in church-related vocations" or "women in ministry," while many others regarded the term "ministry" as being pastoral. Following that meeting, the WMU at its annual meeting held a dinner for women in ministry and invited missionary women so they would know that they were included.

The WMU took a big step in 1982, the year of the seventy-fifth anniversary of the Woman's Missionary Union Training School, which was then the Carver School of Missions and Social Work at Southern Baptist Theological Seminary. C. Anne Davis, professor at Carver, was the major speaker. Sarah Frances Anders, a graduate of the training school and professor at Louisiana College, also was featured. She reported on her research on women in the ministry in the SBC. As the women enjoyed the fellowship with each other, and as they listened to testimonies from leading women, it was evident that something needed to be done to provide support for these women. In 1983, in Louisville, Kentucky, a group of women met to discuss what kind of organization should be created. Thus was born Southern Baptist Women in Ministry, with Southern being deleted in 1993. The organization is now known as Baptist Women in Ministry (BWIM).

The WMU for several years provided a meeting time and place for this group during its annual meeting. In 2003 the twentieth anniversary of BWIM was celebrated in connection with the Cooperative Baptist Fellowship (CBF) General Assembly. Among the "founding mothers" in attendance was Mrs. Frank Stagg, whom I later called Evelyn. The wife of my favorite New Testament professor, Evelyn continues to this day, even in her nineties, to be my friend and mentor. At the present time, BWIM is in a state of revitalization, updating its focus to meet the needs of the woman in ministry today.

At the request from the officers of the Baptist Medical/Dental Fellowship, the WMU led in beginning another organization, the Baptist Nursing Fellowship, which also has celebrated its twentieth anniversary. Although there are men nurses, the doctors felt that the WMU could lead in setting up an organization that would focus on the nursing profession, rather than having them in the larger group of doctors and dentists. Although the nurses continued to meet in connection with the BM/DF, they had their own officers, and June Whitlow, of the WMU staff, served as their executive.

As the 1980s approached, the SBC became even less willing to support women in ministry. The convention resolutions on women became more specific, the criticism of vocal women more stringent. On two occasions, I was contacted by wives of men who later became convention presidents. The first call came from one who responded to my *Total Woman* speech. She started to identify herself to me, and I said, "Oh, yes. We know each other. Remember...." Her call was to tell me that she had no problem bowing to her husband. "I have loved him since high school. I have no problem being submissive to him," she said. "But," I responded, "I have no husband. Must I be submissive to yours?"

On the second occasion, the other pastor's wife visited me. She suggested that she would like to host an event with wives of other pastors, during which they could personally discuss with me my stance. My response to her was, "I would be glad to host such a meeting, at the WMU's building, where they can see what we are about." That never happened. In the conversation, however, she said that through Bible study she had come to realize it was all right for me to head the WMU, but she could not, scripturally, because it would place her in a position higher than her husband's.

During my seven years as the WMU executive in Florida and my fifteen years in the national office, I was a frequent guest in pulpits. Often I was listed as speaker. Sometimes my topic would be listed as the "message." My motto became, "Call it anything you want to, just let me do it." I often encountered opposition when I went into churches to preach. In a church in Florida, following my Sunday morning "message," I was approached by a young man. With his Bible open, he stated his objections to my being in the pulpit, "usurping the place of the pastor." I assured him that I had been invited by the pastor and that I had not usurped his place. Later, that young man wrote a very nice, apologetic letter, assuring me that he was a new Christian and that he had a lot to learn.

In a state evangelism meeting, at which I was the keynote evening speaker, the presiding pastor said, "Brethren (to a mixed crowd containing 'sistren'), my Bible says, 'Let the women keep silent in the church. If they have questions, let them ask their husbands.' Our next speaker is Carolyn Weatherford." As I stood at the pulpit, I turned to him, smiled, and said, "Brother, my Bible says the same thing. But I don't have a husband." The congregation laughed and applauded.

At a state convention meeting, I was the final speaker of the evening. The state executive turned to me and said, "Carolyn, I hate to tell you this, but a lot of folks don't like it that I've invited you to speak to the convention." I assured him that it was okay with me. The speaker/preacher before me, however, read his text, Matthew 28:1. His entire message related to those foolish women who "went to look at the tomb." The Christ had risen, but those foolish women only went to look at the tomb. It was impossible for me not to refer to the rest of the chapter, however, without openly defying him, when I stood to deliver my message.

While I have faced opposition, I have also received great encouragement and support. All along the way, I have been blessed by people who have encouraged, pushed, guided, and blessed me. In my hometown of Frostproof, my mother headed the list, along with my deacon daddy. Mrs. Edwards, who led the GAs, Gwen Boyette, my biology teacher and a strong leader in my church, and Nell and Curt Clements were my role models. Elizabeth Provence, the WMU young people's secretary, was, and continued to be until her death several years ago, the outstanding influence in my becoming the woman that I am. We referred to each other as Paul and Timothy because we did not know of a female mentor/mentee team in the Bible.

While in college, I grew under the tutelage of my BSU director, Faith James (now Faith Butler, living in Colorado). A woman in my church, "Mom Tully," became, through the WMU in the church, my "foster parent," a ministry that the WMU provided through the BSU. Mrs. Tully, a widow, was a juvenile worker in the county court system. She was a dear friend and guide through the years. I listened to her philosophy of life and watched as she lived it out. In my days in Tampa, Ella Gaventa was my major influence. Mrs. Gaventa, a widow and the mother of the missionary doctor William Gaventa, showed me in her own quiet way what it meant to be a leader.

In seminary, Helen Falls and Sibyl Townsend were my role models and mentors. Another role model was Harriett Mather, the sister of Juliette Mather, a long-time WMU youth worker, and of Ruth Mather, an American Baptist missionary to India. Harriett became someone I wanted to follow.

Then, during my thirty-one years in the WMU, I had numerous role models. Josephine Jones, my "boss" when I was GA director and whom I succeeded when she retired as executive director, showed me how to be a real Southern Christian lady. In many ways, I followed her pattern for years. My first WMU "boss" was Mary Essie Stephens in Alabama. Always demanding the best of her employees, she was also an encourager and a teacher. Among other WMU leaders, the name of Marie Mathis shines in my heart. As I watched her preside over the national WMU board meetings, as I listened to her wise counsel, and as I watched her interchange with all kinds of people, I thought, "I want to be like Mrs. Mathis." My life has never been barren of wonderful women who helped me.

I have also received encouragement from my home churches. In 1984, when Vestavia Hills Baptist Church, my church in Birmingham, Alabama, decided that it was time to elect women deacons, my pastor Otis Brooks encouraged me to accept the nomination. I declined for two reasons. Because of my heavy travel schedule, I felt that I could not carry out the stated functions of a deacon, and accepting ordination as a deacon was not a battle I wanted to give my energies to at that time. I encouraged the women who were selected, and in my church they were well received.

Much of my time as the leader of the national WMU was spent in the air. Courtesy of the Home Mission Board, I visited home missionaries in every state. I learned of their work and provided encouragement and often counseling for them. Courtesy of the Foreign Mission Board, I was invited to visit foreign missionaries in almost 100 countries. It was a special privilege to observe the work of the women missionaries and to see how the national Christian women were serving. Surprisingly, I saw some of these women preaching and pastoring churches.

During the early days of women's ordination among Southern Baptists, I witnessed the ordination to the ministry of two women. Aline Fuselier was already on the staff of the WMU when I arrived in Birmingham. I had a strong appreciation for her gifts, and somehow I was not surprised when she asked to talk with me. She came to my home, and as we lolled in the swimming pool, she told me that she wanted to be ordained and that her church had agreed to ordain her. She became the first employee of the WMU to be ordained. I am happy to say that she is still busy, with her husband, as a minister. Another young woman, Mary Price, was the daughter-in-law of friends, and I also knew her parents. Her father was a long-time director of missions in Alabama. Mary was ordained by University Baptist Church in Montevallo, the church she attended while in college. I attended the service, and through the years I have followed her life. She is a chaplain, supervises clinical pastoral education students, travels to lead conferences, advocates for chaplains, and counsels with women in ministry. I also have followed the work of University Baptist Church. Its current pastor is a woman, Robin Nosworthy. Since Mary's ordination, I have participated in, or simply attended, the ordination of a number of women. The number is growing, and I am grateful.

I finally did get to China. When the WMU was preparing to celebrate its centennial in 1988, under the leadership of Catherine Allen, we developed the "Lottie Moon Tours of China." I led one of the first groups. My life seemed to have gone the full circle from that day in the back yard in Frostproof. But, no, there was life after China.

In 1989 I married J. Joseph Crumpler, who had been a pastor in Ohio for about thirty years. He had gone with his first wife and small son to Defiance, Ohio, following seminary and had remained in that state. His wife died in 1982, and when I visited Ohio in 1983 to speak at the annual meeting of the State Convention of Baptists in Ohio, the state WMU executive asked him to take me to dinner. For several years we dated in full view of the world, and finally, with the celebration of the 100th anniversary of the WMU complete and Joe's last child out of college, we married.

Several months after our wedding trip to Europe, I was approached by Daniel Vestal, who was going to run for the SBC presidency. He wanted me to run as first vice president. As I struggled with the decision, Joe said, "You must do it. You have a lot of information now that you will not have in years to come. Do it!" So, for about six months, I traveled the country with Daniel and Steve Tondera, a Baptist layman from Huntsville, Alabama, who was running for second vice president. The rest is history, for in 1990, in New Orleans, we were defeated. The defeat was not as devastating as the criticism that I faced when I decided to make the run. The WMU made an official announcement that it had not endorsed my candidacy. I had not asked for the organization's endorsement. I also received letters and phone calls. One letter said, "I can't believe that all these years we let you run the WMU and you don't believe the first five books of the Bible!" Where did the letter writer get that idea?

My life in the parsonage was quite different than my life in the WMU. I learned that all those things I enjoyed talking about were real work. I found out who prepared the beautiful meals and made all the arrangements for my speaking engagements. I spent a lot of time cooking, serving, and entertaining. I love being a pastor's wife. Since his retirement, Joe has continued his ministry as an interim pastor, and I have continued to enjoy my role as pastor's wife.

Eventually, I was ordained a deacon and discovered that my gifts and natural abilities were a perfect fit for that position. I have continued to receive invitations to speak in Sunday morning worship services, and I have continued to be criticized for doing so. But I am grateful for the pastors and churches that have faced the criticism and still invited me to join them in worship. I continue to have a story to tell. I have not felt the need, nor have I had the desire, to be "ordained to the ministry," but I do feel that I am a "woman in ministry." My ministry today is much different from what it was before marriage.

I found a wonderful home in the CBF, a moderate Baptist organization in which Joe and I have participated since its beginning. I served as the fourth moderator. I also served two years as a part-time employee of the North American Baptist Fellowship, a regional organization of the Baptist World Alliance. Yet my service with that organization brought criticism from those who confused it with CBF. I have served on various boards formed by "new Baptists"—*Baptists Today*, the Baptist Center for Ethics, *Christian Ethics Today*, Friends of New Churches, and the CBF Foundation. I was elected to another term on the BWIM board, and I was one of the founding members of Global Women, a new organization focused on the needs of women in the world and the gifts of young women in the United States who do not have a place where their services and their calling are effectively utilized. I continue in my service as trustee of the American Bible Society, where I currently am the recording secretary and in my twentieth-fifth year of service.

But most exciting is my own personal, local ministry. In my first month as pastor's wife, I was approached by a young woman who was working with Mission Friends in the church. She asked me if I would be her mentor. She wanted to learn how to be a more effective Christian. After leading a conference in an area WMU workshop, I was approached by another young woman who asked if she could learn from me. These two mentorships are still in place today, and I have had the joy of seeing these two women grow into spiritual maturity.

At the beginning of my courtship with Joe, I met Vera and Velma, two elderly sisters in his church who had never married and who had no family. I began to run errands for them, giving "Pastor Joe" time for other ministries. Vera and Velma became my dear friends. They have since died, and other older women have come into my life whom I now can serve: Viola, Myrle, Evelyn, Myrtle, Beryl, Josephine, and the list grows.

In recent years, two local ministries grabbed my heart and mind. God's Home for Families was begun by a Baptist social worker who realized that there were various social agencies to help boys, girls, men, and women, but she had no place of referral for families in need. She left her job and began God's Home for Families. Joe had been on her board, and soon I became a member as well. The other ministry, Lydia's House, provides help to children infected/affected by AIDS. This ministry began in the late 1990s, and I serve on its board.

Being a grandma is my all-time favorite ministry. Joe has three children, and we now have four grandchildren. All four have made professions of faith and are active in church groups. Once our granddaughter Abby was studying about itinerant preachers, and she said, "Isn't that what Grandma was?" What will these children be in the future? The Lord knows. The assurance that I have is that if God calls any one of them—the two boys or the two girls—they will be ready to say, "Here I am, Lord." As one of the boys said when he was five or six, "God can call anybody he wants to be a preacher!"

Many of our friends have left the Baptist denomination. We considered the possibility. Then we determined that we are Baptist in our hearts. We are focused on being Christian first and then on being free and faithful Baptists, joining hands with other like-minded Baptists to continue the work begun so long ago.

A Southern Baptist pastor friend called several years ago, and he said, "Carolyn, I am so sorry that we lost you." My response was, "You didn't lose me; you just dismissed me." Am I sad? Not any longer. I have found that there is life beyond the Southern Baptist Convention, in a wide circle of Baptists committed to being the presence of Christ in the world today.

CHAPTER 5

# "The Call Does Not Stop, For New Avenues of Ministry Keep Opening Up"

### SUE FITZGERALD

"I do not know what God wants me to do," I said to my mother during the summer after my first year in college. Her answer came quickly, "Have you prayed?" I assured her that I had, and she said, "Then don't worry about it."

That conversation has stuck in my mind through the years. Feeling God's presence, I have prayed, listened, and moved one step at a time into the future, letting God guide me. Another conversation with my father had the same impact on my life. He said to me one day, "Daughter, I don't know where you will be in the future, whether in Africa or somewhere right here at home. You can do anything you want to do." His words were the support and blessing I needed as I sought to find God's call for my life.

A creative mother who did not see obstacles but rather challenges and a listening father who was always ready to help others were both strong mentors. Both were strong, gentle teachers and leaders who drew people to them in church and community. They could laugh even in difficult situations and cry in joy or in sorrow. They allowed me to be critical but always expected me to look at the other side of any situation.

Their strength came from a faith that began in prayer. Each morning in our home in Gretna, Virginia, they began the day on their knees in prayer. Each evening my father sang on the way up the stairs and once again before getting into bed, they both were on their knees to pray. In our home, after supper we had family devotional time, and anyone visiting us was invited to join us. We four children learned to read the Bible and pray during this important family time. As each of us left home, we knew the family was praying for us at suppertime. Three things that I learned from my parents stand out as guiding my whole ministry: keep praying, keep listening, and keep growing.

One experience confirmed these principles. While I was a student at Meredith College in Raleigh, North Carolina, I returned home one weekend and drove my father to a rural church that was having a deacon ordination service. Daddy had been invited to pray the ordination prayer for a man whom he had befriended. On the way, he said to me, "I want you to help me learn to pray better."

In addition to my mother, we had other strong women in our family who had a lasting impact on my life. Before women were considered for ordination, Aunt Mary said to me, "Sue, you need to be ordained." Aunt Susie taught the nursery children for fifty years, and yet she wanted me to come back from college and give her new ideas for her nursery work. Her ministry in the community was to help all the new mothers in town and all her "old critters," as she called the older ladies, most of whom were younger than she was. Aunt Frances was a deacon in my home Baptist church before I was born in 1931. She rotated off the deacon board in 1950. (Rotation of deacons began around this time.) When I went to seminary, Aunt Frances supported me verbally as well as by giving me a little money each fall. That small amount of money was like a comfort blanket, reminding me of her love and prayers. Aunt Gertrude showed me by example that the call of God is a growing, changing experience. She moved from one area of ministry to another as life changed and new opportunities presented themselves. Another mentor, the wife of our minister in Gretna, was a creative teacher in Sunday School and in Bible school where we had a good time while learning a great deal.

God's call to me was not to a specific task but to movement through open doors. Some of these were major decisions, such as accepting a job in a specific place. Other doors through which I walked could only be seen in retrospect when reflecting on God's guidance. One example of this was knowing Ruth Beckwith, an African American with whom I worked in the cafeteria during college days. Each day when I went to work after class, she expected me to tell her what I had learned. Sitting together on the city bus in the days before integration, she taught me about racial problems. Praying, listening, and being willing to try new ventures made me open to God's call and also caused me apprehension and excitement because I never took a job that was not more challenging than the previous job.

In 1952, after I graduated with a religion degree from Meredith, I began teaching weekday religious education classes in the public schools in Blacksburg, Virginia. Each week I taught twenty-one different classes and had students in grades one through seven. Seventeen classes were in the white town school, two were in a two-room rural school, and two were in the African American school. The curriculum, developed by the Virginia Council of Churches, covered Old and New Testaments, development of the Bible, church history, and appropriate subjects for grades one through three. As I began teaching these classes, I realized how little I knew about the Bible and wished that I had been taught more in Sunday School. My limited knowledge made me work harder, teaching in-depth in each course and testing to see how far down in the grades I could teach big ideas. Visiting the churches that the students attended gave me a realistic view of the small rural church and stimulated my desire to work in small churches, helping them through education.

I was expected to have a year-end program in each school. Although this occurred before integration, it did not seem right to have a separate program for each school, so in May 1953 Blacksburg had its first integrated program, and without an incident. This experience made me realize that helping students grow is possible if I was willing to go slowly, plan carefully, and let God work through me as I helped children face their prejudices.

Before the year was up, I received a call from the First Baptist Church, Lynchburg, Virginia, to work in education and with youth. As I considered the call, I asked the minister whether he wanted someone creative or just someone to grease the wheels. He assured me that he would support a creative ministry.

With much prayer and soul searching, I finally put the fleece out to God. "If you want me to go, tell me by morning," I told God. I awakened with Genesis 12:1 ringing in my head: "Get thee out of thy country to a land I will show thee." The call was clear, and in the summer of 1953 I began my work in Lynchburg.

The church was open for me to be creative. Still strong in my mind was the weakness of church literature. The desire for better literature led me to develop a two-year cycle of study for grades one through twelve. My curriculum combined the work being done in Training Union (the Sunday evening program) and the youth mission education programs. Some of the courses of study were Old and New Testaments, missions, church history, the development of the Bible, ethics, and theology, all designed with the appropriate age level in mind.

As I look back at my three years in Lynchburg, I realize that I learned a great deal about leadership. One can influence people to do new things and accept change, but it is much more difficult to lead persons to think through issues so that change comes because they want it, not because the leader wants it. That kind of change is internal and will last even when a new paid staff member comes to the church.

The work in Lynchburg stretched me and helped me grow. I realized that more education was essential if I wanted to continue writing curriculum, so I enrolled at Andover Newton Theological School in Newton Centre, Massachusetts. Andover was the right seminary for me for several reasons. The school accepted women in the Bachelor of Divinity (now Master of Divinity) degree program without a fight, had a course in writing church literature, and was committed to working with each student in planning course studies.

The three years I spent in Massachusetts (1956–1959) were not easy. I was forced to stretch and grow. As a Southerner and a Baptist, I was pushed and confronted by people who saw both labels as narrow. My Southern accent gave me away wherever I went. I was confronted about the race riots that were taking place in the South, which caused me to look honestly at my own background. The course work was difficult and rewarding, and the interaction with students from all over the world and from various denominations opened my vision to the larger church and gave me broader perspective for ministry when I returned to the South to work.

Franklin Baptist Church, Franklin, Virginia, was my first call after seminary. Past experiences and new educational tools gave me the impetus to try new things. One venture was to organize a four-month teacher training program each spring and fall on Sunday morning for twelve to fifteen teachers or potential teachers. This program included serious Bible study using varied teaching methods.

Having studied all kinds of church literature in seminary, I was able to develop a much more open educational program with leaders making decisions related to literature choices that were biblically, theologically, and educationally sound.

My four years in Franklin (1959–1963) helped me grow in leadership ability in three ways: teaching people who want to learn, guiding others in developing leadership skills, and developing the personal skills of working with leadership in the church and community. Church leaders, no matter how educated or uneducated, rich or poor, powerful or powerless, are not the determiners of a church member's conscience. Each decision must be tested by the leadership of Christ.

Still strong was the call to work in small churches, leading me to send out feelers that eventually led to a position at Mars Hill Baptist

Church, Mars Hill, North Carolina. I began working there in the spring of 1963. Mars Hill is a small college town, so I began to work with town-and-gown challenges as well as with students and the larger community.

Early emphases of my ministry were teaching, working with and developing leaders, and guiding literature choices. The Mars Hill church was ready to look at and evaluate existing literature, which meant helping church members develop new skills in making choices. Before making decisions, they looked at literature from different denominations to see that it was sound theologically, biblically, and educationally.

My joy in teaching grew as I worked with different ages from youth through adults. A morning study group composed mostly of senior adults was started and continued for twelve years, studying any topic they chose that related to the faith. In one of the classes while studying a difficult topic, one woman said, "Never heard that before. Keep going!" For the college students, I designed elective choices that included studying books that were controversial. Developing student leadership was accomplished through interns who worked with me in the youth and college programs.

Vacation Bible School was a good time for children and youth to explore topics that they did not get anywhere else, such as worship, church history, ethics, and an overview of the Old Testament. Since there was no literature written on these topics for Vacation Bible School, I developed my own, and the teachers and children had a good time.

In 1967 I began teaching in the extension program sponsored by the six Southern Baptist seminaries. I taught two courses a year. This experience helped a little to satisfy my need to work with small church leadership. Also in the late 1960s I led the Mars Hill church to develop programs for handicapped children and adults living in our county. Volunteers staffed this venture until we obtained grant money and were able to hire a paid staff. Through these programs, we provided education, job training, and work programs. Many of the handicapped people we served went on to find paid jobs at the college cafeteria or in local restaurants. The church continued this ministry for more than twenty years, until it ran into opposition from a local mental health organization.

My experience with pastoral work grew as I spent more time counseling and visiting the sick. Preaching opportunities were always there and increased during the interim times between pastors. "Never heard a woman preach" and "never had a woman serve me communion" were common remarks.

My expanded ministry led directly to the question and struggle with ordination. In seminary the issue arose, but I decided that all are called and all are ministers, thus ordination was not necessary for anyone, male or female. During my years of service at Mars Hill Baptist Church, ordination became much more of an issue as I did more preaching, funerals, and pastoral work but had to refuse weddings because of the lack of credentials. One strong woman in the church said to me, "You are a minister." Later, I found that most of the people assumed that I was already ordained since I did almost every task in the church at one time or another.

With prayer, listening, studying, and a willingness to grow, I once again "put out the fleece." "God," I prayed, "if you want me to be ordained, let the church ask me." In peace, I quit struggling. It was not long before the church asked if it could ordain me. I said yes to God and to the church, and on May 5, 1973 I was ordained. Banners made by the children and youth adorned the church sanctuary. With my mother and father attending, the service included participation from all ages, races, and various denominations.

Ordination was not the beginning of the call, but only the capstone of what had happened all through the years. The road to that day was paved with the silent yeses to God and the open answers to calls to leadership in little and big places. It was the willingness to change and be led by God through the church. Ordination is a three-way process: God calls, the church ratifies the call, and the person must answer.

Still I dreamed of a broader ministry to small churches. Plan after plan was put in a file. The file grew, but there was no response to letters written or conferences with people as to the value of such a ministry. Knowing that it was possible, I continued to pray and listen for any opening that might lead to a wider ministry.

The opportunity came when Fred Bentley, president of Mars Hill College, mentioned at a luncheon meeting that he wanted to develop a ministry to churches in Western North Carolina. I let him know that I already had a plan. He asked me to meet him in his office the next morning to talk about it. The plan was polished that night and handed to him the next morning. He liked the plan and said that he was willing to try it on a half-time basis, which I refused. It needed to be full time or not at all. His reply was, "Maybe it won't work, and you will be out of a job." I assured him that it would work. I resigned my position at Mars Hill Baptist Church, and I opened the doors of the Center for Christian Education Ministries in 1975. I spent the next twenty years praying, listening, serving, and growing as I ministered all over Western North Carolina through preaching, teaching, leading workshops, counseling, and being present for pastors and leaders who needed new ideas, materials, or just a listening ear.

The center's purpose was to help pastors and church leaders in Western North Carolina through resources, leadership, and ideas. Located in the old bookstore and snack bar, the center had plenty of room for materials pertaining to every area of church life. One large section contained commentaries, Bible studies, and books relating to church history, theology, and ethics. Other sections of literature in the center were well defined, enabling a pastor to browse and find needed materials. There were resources related to church administration, family life, Christian education, drama, evangelism, missions, children, music, counseling, recreation, stewardship, and youth work. The center also had audiovisual aids of every kind. Any of these resources could be checked out. The use of the center varied from year to year, but each year approximately 400 persons checked out between 1,500 to 2,000 items.

The center also had samples of literature from different denominations that could be perused to find the right study for a church or a class. Many pastors and church leaders did not know all the available literature from their own denomination, much less that of other denominations. At associational meetings I set up displays, and in many churches I led workshops so that leaders could see the types of literature available. Such workshops included ideas about decision-making related to their own church literature needs. Sometimes this meant developing literature for a small church when the convention's literature was written with a larger church in mind. It meant listening to needs and being open to new answers to meet those needs.

The center not only provided resources for churches and associations but also helped to meet specific needs. In addition to literature workshops, I also taught classes on specific studies on the Bible, church history, Baptist history and beliefs, teacher training, grief and death, and deacon leadership. I also led prayer retreats.

Ministering to the churches in Western North Carolina was rewarding, especially my teaching of seminary extension classes in four different associations. The classes, developed in conjunction with the Baptist seminaries, required eighteen hours in the classroom over a nine-week period. In twenty-seven years, I taught over seventy-five classes including courses in the Old and New Testaments, church history, Baptist history, theology, ethics, and Christian education. Some specific courses I taught were Dynamics of Teaching, Public Worship, Formation for Ministry, and Leadership in the Small Church. Every class was a challenge to help each student in his or her area of need. For example, in one class I had a minister who had only a third-grade education and another who had a seminary degree. Many students came to class with the idea that they should only use the King James Version of the Bible, yet they came and wanted to learn. My philosophy was to go slowly, be gentle, simplify but never distort the truth, and let them know that each one had to think and make his or her own decisions. Often I provided extra books if the textbook was too difficult. One minister, who probably had taken as many as twenty courses with me, introduced me to his church as one who had taught him to think.

Another purpose of the center was to help church leaders with new ideas. When leaders came to the center for help, I felt that one important task was to give them ideas so that they could solve their own problems. Most everyone is creative. My philosophy is that if I give a person ten ideas, he or she will come up with the eleventh, the best one for a given problem.

Working at the college, I had the privilege of teaching Christian education courses as well as leading students through an internship program. Each semester four to six students registered for the intern program in the Center for Christian Education Ministries. Only students who wanted to be challenged and to grow were accepted in the rigorous program. Each student worked in the center and studied one specific area of ministry. Seeing students grow and take leadership roles that they had not dreamed possible was rewarding. One example comes to mind. In a role-play situation I called one young lady a minister. She let me know that she was not a minister. A few years later I had the opportunity to preach at her ordination service. The growing was not one way, for students also challenged me. Together we struggled with issues, listened to each other, and sought to find God's word for the needs of the day.

The work at the center was rewarding as I helped people when they came to our building. I also attended associational meetings and preached and taught in many churches all over Western North Carolina. Each day had new open doors of opportunities that needed to met, for open doors often closed at a later time.

Mars Hill Baptist Church asked me to serve as interim pastor in 1994. For the next year I worked half-time at the center and almost full-time at the church. During that year of interim work, I did much of the preaching for the church and all the pastoral care work, including nineteen funerals.

In 1995 I retired from Mars Hill College, but not from ministry. To continue my ministry, my carport was enclosed and made into a library. Ministers and church leaders come and use the materials and receive personal counsel. I continue to grow and hear the call of God. The call does not stop, for new avenues of ministry keep opening up as I am able to hear. As in the beginning, it still takes prayer, listening, and the willingness to grow.

Ministry in the South as a woman has not been easy, especially among Baptists. I had to overcome roadblocks. The first roadblock consisted of the reactions of individuals to me. Some reactions were to me as a strong woman and others to my position as an ordained woman. Many persons, both men and women, cannot relate to a strong female. The answer to this obstacle is knowing oneself well enough to discern when to be gentle and when to be tough. Jesus said it this way: "Be wise as serpents and innocent as doves." Sometimes I made mistakes and had to apologize for being too tough. Once I was too tough with members of a youth group and had to apologize to them later. Their reply was, "Yes, we recognized that you were just trying to mother us."

A few ministers, educated and uneducated, expressed fear by wanting to remove me from whatever position I had with them. Some laymen followed their minister's advice never to listen to a woman preach by walking out when I started to preach. Other ministers treated a female as someone limited in intelligence, but a good theological or serious question about their church usually helped move their thinking to a different level. This same approach was the one I used when I felt that I was a victim of sexism.

As to being an ordained female, I encountered many barriers along the way. Often it would have been easy to listen to those negative words, if I had let fear take over. Before I was ordained, one associational missionary said to me, "You are going to ruin yourself." I chose not to reply in words or in body language, and I continued to work with him for many years. While visiting him in the hospital in his later years, he said to me, "Sue, you are more of a minister to me than all the rest of them." Other leaders in associational work poured out their problems to me when they came to the center, but they would not recognize me and often ignored me when I spoke at their associational meeting.

On the church level, in preaching, teaching, or leading workshops, the ministers more than the lay persons expressed their feelings about me. The following introduction in one church expressed the minister's feelings: "I do not agree with her, but she has helped us." One minister even prayed at a funeral that we were conducting together: "O Lord, you know we do not agree with what is going on here today." Another time, after I had preached in a church, the minister expressed his fear as we walked to the back of the church at the end of the service: "I am afraid you are going to take over my job."

The reactions of individuals can be an obstacle, but systems present obstacles as well. The association is one system that has had to filter or to work through male ministers' problems with female ministers. One association had a called meeting concerning my participation in its annual meeting because the minister of the host church said that I would not be welcomed to speak in his church. To spare my feelings, the association asked me not to come. I let them know that this was all right, for I would be there anyway since my name was already on the printed program. Prior to that meeting, I had been in many of the association's meetings and even preached in some of association's churches without any problems.

The Southern Baptist Convention has become a major hindrance, requiring teachers in the seminary extension program to sign the 2000 *Baptist Faith and Message*, which blocks my further teaching in that program. Action in the convention has made ministers back off and ride the fence on many issues, including issues relating to women.

One minister who attended a seminary extension class forbade his church members from taking any classes with me. He said, "If anyone teaches you, I will." The members did not attend any more classes, but they continued to come to me for help in every area of church life. That minister's fear of my teaching did not stop our mutual friendship, which lasted until his death.

A personal problem for me has been physical pain resulting from college sports injuries. Often the pain would get the best of me, but continued prayer has helped me through hard days and long nights. When my body was in trouble, God's help was sufficient, always providing me with what I needed. When in pain while counseling students, I managed by praying for the other person. I also prayed for myself that I would listen compassionately. Pain and a cane were assets in ministry in a strange way.

Handling adversity is a challenge, and how a person meets that challenge determines the health of the person as well as the depth of ministry. When facing adversity, I believe that personhood is the place to start. I must first accept my own personhood as uniquely created by God with special gifts, and, with God's call, to use those gifts in the way that will bring glory to God and joy to others as well as to myself. I am first a person and then a female. I express my personhood through my femaleness. When a unique person can live and work in joy, then God can say "Amen" to that particular creation. The discovery of gifts is a lifetime task, for each new turn in the road opens unexplored avenues of self, as well as new ways to minister through the growing self.

Self-discovery is not exclusively done by my own analysis, but rather through prayer and through insights that others offer, forcing me to look honestly at myself. So often these come through challenges that can either stunt my growth or allow me to see myself in a fresh way that turns a negative into a positive.

For example, after the minister prayed negatively about me at the funeral, my first reaction was to laugh, but that passed. I thought through what I did wrong in that particular situation that made him react in a hidden (eyes closed in prayer) yet public way (loud for all to hear). It gave me new understandings as to how I should serve with ministers like him who have been taught to oppose women ministers. I used those new insights when serving with other ministers. At another funeral the minister leaned over to me and said, "You know, Sue, I respect you." Working with him again at a second funeral, he said, "Sue, you go first and I will be last. If the two ministers in between us talk too long, I will cut my part short."

Understanding and accepting my personhood is the first way to face roadblocks. The second way is to understand the other person. Just as I must accept my unique self with my own quirks, so I must accept the other person with his or her own uniqueness. That other person's built-in feelings about God, the Bible, the church, the community, and women affect how he or she reacts to me. That person's feelings are his or her business, and how I act or react to that person is my business. I must take other persons seriously, looking them in the eye while listening, praying, and responding. Whether I act or react is up to me and determines the effectiveness of my ministry to that person.

Listening to the other person is central. For example, the minister in my seminary extension class who had only a third grade education was fearful when he found there were tests to take and papers to write. I heard his problem and let him know that I had problems with spelling and that he should not worry about how he wrote. Our friendship lasted until his death.

The third important way to approach a stumbling block is to realize that one cannot change another person. Change comes from within a person and is between that person and God. My job is to listen and offer people new ideas and tools and support them with prayers and love so that they can grow in their area of need. In teaching, my philosophy has been to put one foot where the students are and one foot in front of them.

The fourth way that keeps obstructions from impeding growth is to realize that, as my daddy said, "Sometimes you have to go around

Robinhood's barn to get there." God is not in the business of keeping time on one's ministry. God gives us unique gifts and plants ideas in us but does not have a timetable. To fulfill a dream does not mean doing it the moment the dream comes to the forefront of one's thinking. As God said to Habakkuk, "It may seem slow in coming, but wait for it." (TEV) To make it a reality may require years, but the ensuing time is part of the valuable education toward the fruition of the dream. For example, it took years before I realized the dream of a broader ministry to small churches, but each year of continued service helped prepare me toward the fulfillment of the dream.

God does not have a timetable for us, and God does not expect us to do all the work. As Paul said, "I plant, Apollos waters, and God gives the increase." Being fruitful in the planting is what is important. It is essential to realize that the focus in planting seed is to the person, not to the masses, for each person must separately respond to God. This is a fact whether the work is in teaching, preaching, conducting weddings or funerals, as well as in pastoral work, administrative tasks, or everyday life in the community.

This truth was brought home to me one day when I was at the post office. With mail in hand, I approached my car. A woman whom I did not know stuck her head out of a well-worn car next to mine and spoke to me. She said, "Every time I see you, God speaks to me."

Another important asset for meeting difficulties is a sense of humor. This was exemplified to us as children growing up, for our parents could see the amusing side of most issues. Even when our mother died, we smiled in the midst of tears. The doctor had said that she would not live through the night on February 28. We felt she chose to wait until February 29, a day that comes around only every four years. A sense of humor has helped me through many difficult moments in ministry.

The last way to meet barriers surrounds and permeates all other ways. It is the willingness to struggle with God and self, and to be open to find new approaches for solving problems. This kind of struggle is exciting because it means new ideas as well as internal growth in relationship to God, to self, and to others. This struggle is also frightening, for it opens new doors of ministry.

My ministry has been mainly among Baptists, and some have given me problems, so why have I remained a Baptist? I hold strongly to the Baptist beliefs in the congregational form of government, the autonomy of the local church, the priesthood of believers, believer's baptism, and the separation of church and state. As these are strong beliefs in other denominations, there must be other reasons to remain a Baptist.

I grew up in a Baptist home and in a community that was ecumenical. There were four churches in my hometown, and for many years there were no full-time ministers. For worship each Sunday morning we attended the church that had a service that week. The youth program in town was for all youth. My mother grew up in the Christian Church (Disciples of Christ), and her influence also made me more open to other denominations. A final factor contributing to my ecumenical outlook was my seminary experience. Attending Andover Newton Theological School, where students came from many denominations and where women were more accepted, encouraged me to consider alternatives, but my desire to continue working in the South made me stay with the Baptist denomination.

As Baptists in the South have grown more narrow, presenting more problems for women, the question of changing denominations still arises. However, my call is still to serve Western North Carolina churches that are predominately Baptist. Remaining a Baptist has not kept me from ministering to other denominations that needed my help whether in teaching, preaching, or encouraging church-starts.

Although my goal in ministry has not been to receive human awards, recognitions from outside Western North Carolina have affirmed my work in the mountains. In 1978 Southeastern Baptist Theological Seminary in Wake Forest, North Carolina, gave me the first "Citation for Excellence in Christian Ministry." Wake Forest University in Winston-Salem, North Carolina, invited me to preach the baccalaureate sermon and awarded me the Honorary Doctor of Divinity in 1992. Twice I have preached the baccalaureate sermon at Meredith College in Raleigh, North Carolina. I was invited to serve on the founding board of trustees at the Baptist Theological Seminary at Richmond and accepted that invitation gladly.

These have been affirming, but the rewards from persons with whom I worked in Western North Carolina meant even more to me. Affirmations came in unexpected places. After taking a seminary extension course, one minister confessed that he had been taught that education was not good for a minister, that the King James was the only Bible, and that a man should never let a woman teach him. He changed his mind about all three ideas, enrolled in college, graduated with high grades, and has not stopped studying and growing.

Helping ministers start a library has been another of my joys. One pastor's wife said to me, "Sue, it is your fault. Now he surrounds himself with books."

My real satisfaction has been in seeing students become open to new thinking and be willing to try different ministries. I was touched by former students who started the "Fitzgerald-Bean Scholarship" at Mars Hill College. (Marie Bean is a former campus minister.) This scholarship is awarded annually to a woman studying for Christian ministry. It is rewarding to see a minister begin to value education and enroll in college or seminary. It is humbling when the pastor of the small church says, "Sue, you are a minister to me," or former students call and say, "Thank you."

The local region has provided opportunities for service that have been both rewarding and challenging. Some of them include my work as a hospice chaplain and my service with Neighbors In Need, Inc., a crisis ministry; the County Day Care board; and Mountains of Madison, Inc., a program for handicapped adults.

The greatest reward is the Spirit of God moving, stretching, and challenging me in new ways, giving me more creative juices for new types of ministry. The call of God does not stop when one reaches a certain age or when the paid job ceases. God still calls for me to be open, to listen, and to act at the place where my gifts can be used at a given moment. God continues to lead me, giving me new ideas as I am ready to receive them. My prayer is that as long as I live I will be receptive and open to new joys and ministries in God's kingdom.

CHAPTER 6

# "When God Calls People, He Calls Them to 'Preach the Gospel' to Everyone and in All Places"

IDA MAE HAYS

I'll go where You want me to go, dear Lord,
O'er mountain or plain or sea;
I'll say what You want me to say, dear Lord,
I'll be what You want me to be.[1]

Standing in the choir, with perspiration on my brow, tears in my eyes, and a struggle going on in my heart, the Lord spoke to me one Sunday. I could not honestly sing the words, "I'll go where You want me to go, dear Lord." No, Lord, I cannot be a missionary.

I was just fifteen years old. Two years earlier, I had begun attending the Providence Baptist Church (now Second Baptist Church) in West Plains, Missouri. I accepted Christ as my personal Savior at age thirteen and was baptized at age fourteen. Now, God was calling me to be a missionary. There seemed to be so many obstacles in the way: How would my family accept my decision to be a missionary since they were not active in church? Where would I be able to get the resources to go to college and seminary because my parents would not be able to help financially? Could I really do the work of a missionary in a foreign country? But deep down in the very depths of my soul I knew the destiny of my life. I knew that God was in control, that he would give me what it takes to face obstacles with courage and determination, and that he would open the doors at the right moment for me to fulfill his will for my life. My favorite scripture became Philippians 4:13, "I can do all things through Christ who strengthens me," which has been a source of strength throughout my life.

I became even more involved in church activities, Sunday School, Training Union, choir, and Young Woman's Auxiliary (YWA), but the call to missions would not go away. Everywhere I turned, God's still small voice was there: in community missions activities, visitation, a Training Union program, and a weekend at YWA camp.

Between my junior and senior years in high school, at age seventeen, I had the opportunity to spend the summer months working at the Missouri Baptist State Assembly at Hollister Hill, Missouri. My job was waiting the tables in the dining room. During those first three weeks, many missionaries came and went. It seemed that most all of them sat at my tables. It did not take long for me to realize that God also was there. So I decided to interview each missionary in order to find out more about missions. I even took notes, which I still have.

One missionary, Ona Belle Cox, a missionary to Brazil, was there all three weeks. She sat at my table at almost every meal. But I could not bring myself to talk with her. On Saturday evening, July 13, 1957, as I was walking toward the dining room to participate in a staff party, Miss Cox crossed my path. I thought to myself, "If I am ever going to talk with her, I better do it now." So I spoke to her and we sat down on one of the large boulders on top of a mountain overlooking the river. We talked and prayed together. I never got to the staff party that night, but I had a celebration with the Lord. Miss Cox was God's instrument who led me to commit my life to missions that night. It had taken me two years to make that commitment. The next morning, Sunday, I went to the dining room to do my work, but Miss Cox was not there. I inquired about her and was told that she had left early that morning. The night before had been my last chance to talk with Miss Cox, and I had almost missed my opportunity. It was all in God's plan. We corresponded a few times over the years, but I would see her only two other times on her furlough many years later.

Now my heart's desire was just to be a missionary. Everything that I did pointed toward serving overseas. I had no other plans. Obedience to the Lord's claim on my life set into motion a ministry that would impact my life to this very day.

Sharing my call and commitment to missions with my family was not easy. I encountered misunderstanding and opposition. My church, on the other hand, was very supportive. Pearl Webster, my Sunday School teacher and YWA counselor, encouraged me and provided some financial help from time to time with my college and seminary studies and throughout my missionary career. Many times a simple "thank you" seemed so inadequate for all she did.

During my senior year in high school, Mrs. Webster contacted Southwest Baptist College (now University) in Bolivar, Missouri, regarding the possibility of obtaining a scholarship to facilitate my college studies. I knew nothing of this contact until I arrived on the college campus, at which time the president of the college, Dr. John W. Dowdy, offered me a work scholarship that would pay the major expenses for the two years I would be studying there. I lived in the dormitory but worked in the Dowdy's home almost every day. I also helped care for their three boys, and from time to time I assisted Mrs. Dowdy in serving at special functions of the college. Dr. and Mrs. Dowdy taught me so many things and became my "second" parents and special mentors until their deaths.

While at Southwest Baptist College, I was actively involved in missions activities, participated on revival teams to churches in the area, and was involved in all the activities at First Baptist Church, where I was a member. Upon graduation in 1960 with an Associate of

Arts degree, I had planned to go to Howard College (now Samford University) in Birmingham, Alabama. Arrangements were made to live with a family in Birmingham while I attended college there. But after a few days in Birmingham I decided to return home. All the plans I had made to continue college abruptly came to a screeching halt. I was frustrated because what had seemed so right did not work out. The family I was to live with was extremely disappointed as well. It took years for me to understand fully why "my plans" were not God's plans.

Living at home again, under the roof of my parents, was not easy because I had been "on my own" for two years. Some of the good folks in my home church directed comments to me on several occasions: "I thought you said God had called you to be a missionary." "I guess you just made a mistake." "Why did you quit college?" "Why have you come back home?" "What are you going to do now?" Those comments and questions hurt deeply. I finally found a job as a waitress in a downtown restaurant where I worked for six weeks. Then I worked in a dry goods store for about nine months. In March 1961 Dr. Dowdy invited me to return to Southwest Baptist College to work as secretary to the dean and registrar. I accepted the invitation immediately and moved to Bolivar, where I lived and worked for two and a half years.

What seemed to be a "big mistake" and a "long detour" of three years actually became the "testing ground" and preparation for all that God had in his plans for my life. I could not see the reasons for delaying my college studies. It took many years and many times of reflecting on the experiences of those three years to realize God's purpose and the way he led me. Through that detour, God demonstrated his love for me in many, vivid ways. God taught me how to cope with a father who drank, how to deal with a mother's illness, how to overcome timidity and low self-esteem, how to manage finances, how to assume responsibility not only for myself but in the world of business, how to relate and be sensitive to the needs of people in every kind of situation, how to face conflict and not run away from difficulties, and how to learn all kinds of skills that would be useful on the mission field. Most of all, my Christian faith and commitment to missions were deepened, and a courage and determination challenged me to move forward to be obedient to the Lord always. At some point, I came to realize and accept my call to missions as also a call to singleness.

In 1963 I was privileged to meet Fred Wood, a trustee of Union University in Jackson, Tennessee. He took a personal interest in helping me find a job and enroll at Union University. I had already resigned from my position at Southwest Baptist College and was in the process of moving to Jackson when my mother passed away. I almost cancelled my enrollment at the University in order to stay at home again. But at the last minute, I decided to return to Jackson and try to help my father as much as possible from Tennessee. Those were difficult days for all of the family. But a year later my father married again, and the family difficulties lessened.

During my studies at Union, I worked as secretary for the head of the music department as well as an assistant to the dormitory director. Working in a new church start in Jackson provided experience that I would be able to use on the mission field. I became a charter member of the church when it was organized. Julia Walker, my dorm mother whose husband had recently passed away, was especially sensitive to my needs, knowing that I had just lost my mother. Maggie Nell Brewer, dean of women and later vice president of student affairs, became a friend and mentor. Her counsel from time to time was a great encouragement to me. Ann Biggs taught voice and encouraged me to study voice. Because of her encouragement and voice training, I decided to include church music in my seminary studies.

In 1965, upon graduation with a Bachelor of Arts degree in English and Secondary Education, I moved to Fort Worth, Texas, to enroll at Southwestern Baptist Theological Seminary. The four years spent in seminary were meaningful as I more actively prepared myself for missionary service. I studied for the Master of Religious

Education and Church Music degrees, receiving the Master of Religious Education degree in 1968. I never finished the church music degree.

Working as secretary for L. Jack Gray, professor of missions, during those four years at seminary, I became even more aware of missions needs, missionaries, and the work of the Foreign Mission Board (FMB), now the International Mission Board. Dr. and Mrs. Gray and their two daughters became a family to me. Dr. Gray was a mentor who listened, counseled, and encouraged me in my journey toward missionary appointment. Periodically, Edna Frances Dawkins from the personnel department of the FMB came to the campus to interview prospective missionary candidates. Through her guidance I learned about the needs on the different mission fields and, ultimately, began to write my life history, which was a requirement for missionary appointment.

I was involved in many activities at Gambrell Street Baptist Church and at Travis Avenue Baptist Church, which included teaching a junior boys' Sunday School class and singing in the choir. Another couple, Roger and Lavonia Duck, became dear friends. Throughout my missionary career, they would serve as special mentors.

During three summers at seminary, I served as a summer missionary in Maryland with the Home Mission Board and in Virginia with the state Woman's Missionary Union (WMU). I gained experience in working with children and youth in Vacation Bible Schools, working in a social work center, directing Girls' Auxiliary (GA) and YWA camps, and visiting in low-income housing projects.

Toward the end of my last year at seminary I received an invitation to work with the Oklahoma WMU as the state YWA director, which later became the state Acteens director. Knowing that the Missouri Baptist State paper, *Word and Way*, carried an article about my going to Oklahoma, I rushed to the seminary library to read that article. As I opened the *Word and Way*, my eyes fell on a picture of Ona Belle Cox, the missionary who had guided me in my commitment to missions. Miss Cox had passed away. I sensed a great loss in my Christian life. The trauma of the moment caused me to begin considering Brazil as the country where God was calling me to serve.

Working with the Oklahoma WMU (June 1969–August 1971) became the required experience necessary for mission appointment. During those two years, I was in constant contact with the FMB, fulfilling the requirements necessary for appointment and knowing that my missionary assignment would most likely be to work with the WMU in some country. Numerous opportunities gained in Oklahoma provided ample training and experience that helped me: planning, preparing, and leading WMU conferences; directing GA and Acteens camps and retreats; writing leadership materials; meeting national WMU leadership; working closely with the Oklahoma churches; and leading girls and young women to respond to God's call upon their lives.

Finally, on May 11, 1971, at the FMB headquarters in Richmond, Virginia, I realized the fulfillment of the fourteen-year dream of my life: my appointment as a missionary to Brazil. After another four months of missionary orientation, on January 24, 1972, I stepped foot on Brazilian soil.

After a grueling year of Portuguese language study I moved to Recife, Brazil, to begin work with the WMU, in what was then the North Brazil Mission. I was to promote the WMU; direct camps; train girls and women to lead WMU work and to evangelize; prepare leadership materials; and teach a variety of curricula at the WMU seminary in Recife.

After four years I was invited to move to Rio de Janeiro, Brazil, to become the national leader for Baptist Young Women and the secretary of promotion for all of Brazil, working in the national WMU headquarters. For another eight years I traveled all over Brazil promoting the WMU, directing camps, leading conferences, and writing materials for publication. The first responsibility I had when

I arrived in Rio de Janeiro was to write the *Manual for the Baptist Young Women*. Then the Baptist Young Women quarterly magazine, *Missionary Challenge*, was created, which provided ample information and inspiration for the organization of more than 15,000 young women all over the country. By 1984 each Brazilian Baptist young woman was trained to carry on the work as national leader. I felt a great accomplishment in how the Lord had directed my life. The blessings were innumerable.

Making the move from Rio de Janeiro to Brasilia, the national capital of Brazil, became a major transfer in my missions ministry. A new place of service and a different kind of ministry were challenges, and I determined to do my best. Several years were spent doing research and gathering statistics in the Brazil Missions Office located in Brasilia. This responsibility did not seem to be very "missionary," but outside office hours I became involved in several ministries in the Brasilia Baptist State Convention, which enabled me to work closely with Brazilian pastors and churches. I also set up a partnership between the Brasilia Baptist Convention and the Birmingham Baptist Association in Birmingham, Alabama.

Early in 1991, upon my return to Brazil from furlough, I became aware of some existing conflicts and administrative changes that would ultimately, and abruptly, terminate the research and statistics work and my presence in the Brazil Missions Office. I was devastated when it happened. I was told that I had done excellent work and no adequate explanation was made for terminating my position. I came dangerously close to "throwing in the towel" and resigning, until I heard about a derogatory remark a man had made about me. My faith and courage surfaced again and I determined that no one man would keep me from doing God's will. Quietly, but determinedly, I walked through the doors that the Lord opened to ministry and stayed in Brasilia. Years later, that man apologized. Within two years a missionary man was asked to do research and statistics, and the position was recreated.

With the termination of my position, I faced the difficult task of finding another missionary assignment. The Brazilian leadership and the Brasilia Baptist Convention invited me to work as the director of missions and evangelism in the Serrana Association. In that role I visited churches and missions, helped to find pastors for churches, and trained local church leaders. I also assumed the coordination of the partnership between Brasilia and Birmingham. It took almost a year and a half for the International Mission Board (IMB) to approve that new assignment. I was informed that I could not be categorized as a church planter, but only as a church developer. My response was: "That's OK! Call it anything you want. But I assure you that no church can be developed until it is first planted."

The Brasilia/Birmingham partnership included chapel construction and evangelism, and was intended to last for only a three-year period, but it continued for eleven years. From 1990 to 2000, Birmingham volunteers and Brazilian Baptists worked side by side to construct thirty-three chapels and share the gospel. One chapel was constructed at the Brasilia State Baptist Encampment and bears my name: "Prayer Chapel Missionary Ida Mae Hays." Today, Brasilia is the home of strong churches on mission with God to reach the unreached in the center of that great country.

In 1990 my Brazilian pastor confronted me with an unanticipated subject, the ordination of women. We discussed the matter at length. The church where I was a member wanted to ordain me. At that time I told my pastor that I could not permit the church to ordain me, even though I had no problem with women's ordination. I told him that I would have more problems with my missionary colleagues and the IMB than with the Brazilians. I thought the subject was closed, but from 1990 to 2000 my Brazilian pastor asked me every year about ordination.

In the mid-1990s the IMB began to create what would become known as the "New Directions." Drastic administrative changes and field strategies were being put into place by 1997–1998. At one of the annual mission meetings, I heard about all the changes that would take place and determined that I would not stay on the field until I was sixty-five years old but would take early retirement at age sixty-two. I had no desire to spend my last three years in Brazil under that much stress.

Two significant events occurred on the eve of my return to the United States for final furlough and retirement. On January 28, 2001, three weeks before I left Brazil to return to the United States, my pastor and my church planned my ordination as a part of my farewell service. I was unaware of their plans until I arrived at the church. Before an overflowing crowd at the church on that Sunday evening, I knelt on the platform as the pastor prayed and the people present extended their hands toward me, which is a custom in Brazil. I was ordained to the gospel ministry and elected pastor emeritus of the church. I had never sought to be ordained. The church just exercised their autonomous right as a local body of believers.

On February 12, 2001 I found myself in the legislative auditorium of the state legislature of Brasilia. The legislature bestowed upon me the title, "Honorary Citizen of Brasilia" (*Cidadã Honorária de Brasilia*). In that special ceremony it was revealed that I was the second foreigner, the first Baptist missionary in Brasilia, and one of the few women to receive the title.

I returned to the United States on February 19, 2001, for my final furlough and early retirement. I decided to go ahead and retire early primarily because I did not want to have to face the hassle of all the "New Directions," which were being put into place. I did not agree with the changes that were being made, so I just opted out, knowing full well that I would be losing three year's salary, Social Security, and annuity pension benefits.

I settled into the missionary residence of the Lakeside Baptist Church in Birmingham, Alabama. Within the first month I received two gifts from the Birmingham folk: a new automobile and a home. The Lakeside Baptist Church gave me its missionary residence as my retirement home. What a blessing it was to be so genuinely received by the Birmingham folks who had spent eleven years partnering with

Brasilia in the construction of chapels and numerous evangelistic efforts!

After arriving in Birmingham a journalist from *The Birmingham News* interviewed me for a Sunday feature story. Shortly thereafter a journalist from *The Alabama Baptist* interviewed me. Three or four days after that interview, the journalist called to say he had heard that I was ordained and he wanted to verify that fact. I acknowledged that I had been ordained but asked him not to print that in the article. But when the article appeared in *The Alabama Baptist* on April 12, 2001, the journalist had printed information about my ordination. I was concerned, but put the thought aside, since no one questioned me about the matter.

Some time during the early months of my furlough I received a letter from the IMB, as did all the other missionaries, asking all mission board personnel to sign a document of intent to accept and follow the 2000 *Baptist Faith and Message*. I received the letter but did nothing with it. Little did I know that a storm was brewing on the horizon! I had no idea I would be thrust into the middle of a controversy because of my Brazilian ordination.

My concern increased when my Brazilian pastor called in May and shared the details of an anonymous telephone call that he had received from a person, who he believed was a missionary in Brasilia, regarding my ordination. The anonymous caller, whom I know, offended my pastor by using some very ugly terminology in Portuguese and telling my pastor that he would be the cause of my losing my retirement. The caller also made threats to my pastor.

In June I received an unexpected telephone call from the IMB with a summons to meet Robin Hadaway, the regional leader for Brazil, and Johnny Nantz, an IMB trustee, for a meeting in the Atlanta airport on July 20, 2001. The purpose of the meeting was not mentioned, but I suspected that it was about my ordination. Before that meeting Dr. Hadaway never once tried to get in touch with me to ask for an explanation. He did not even follow basic Christian principles of consultation before taking a matter to the next level of consideration. Upon my arrival at the Atlanta airport for the meeting he simply showed me a copy of the article in *The Alabama Baptist*. Without my knowledge he had taken the matter directly to the Eastern South America (ESA) committee of the IMB board of trustees.

Dr. Hadaway told me that he wanted his wife to be present in the meeting along with the IMB trustee. The reason for her presence was never explained. I was questioned for over two hours regarding my ordination, my pastor emeritus status, the 2000 *Baptist Faith and Message*, and other related subjects. At times, I felt like the questioning was actually an interrogation. The trustee, after reading to me the portion of the 2000 Baptist Faith and Message stating that women cannot hold the office of pastor, asked me if I wanted to be a pastor. My response was that at that particular moment I had not given the matter much thought primarily because of my age and because I was looking toward retirement in less than a year. Dr. Hadaway then asked me if I had ever preached. Turning in my chair and facing him, I responded, "Yes, I have preached many, many times." What I really wanted to say, but did not, was: "What does a missionary do if they do not preach, or proclaim, the gospel? Why would I spend half my life in Brazil as a missionary if I did not preach the good news of the gospel?"

Dr. Hadaway then told me that I must respond to the following recommendation that the ESA Committee had prepared: "We recommend that a trustee of the Eastern South America Committee and the Regional Leader ask Ida Mae Hays to publicly rescind her ordination to the gospel ministry and her title of pastor emeritus." The recommendation did not indicate that the wife of the regional leader would be present at the meeting. A copy of the recommendation was not even provided for me; it was merely read to me. But upon my request Dr. Hadaway finally wrote the recommendation on the back of his IMB business card, which I still have in my possession. I was given ten days, until July 31, to prepare a written statement for the trustees. I was told that my response

would be published. (My letter was never published.) As instructed, I
sent the letter to Dr. Hadaway and Rev. Nantz. The portion of the
letter that states my position on the matter is as follows: "Having
reflected upon the above recommendation, and from what I
understand the meaning of the word 'rescind' to be, as the recipient
of the honor, the power to 'rescind' is not mine. Only the giver of the
honor, the First Baptist Church of Paranoá in Brasilia, Brazil, has the
power and authority to 'rescind' or 'recall' that honor."

The trustees met on August 1. I received an e-mail message, one
week later, from Dr. Hadaway, in which he said that they "carefully
considered my response but did not make a decision. The matter
would be considered again at the September 6–8 meeting." After the
September meeting I received an e-mail message from Dr. Hadaway
on September 14, two weeks after the meeting, in which he wrote,
"The committee passed the following statement which was then
approved for publication in the public minutes by the full board.
'The IMB does not recognize the ordination or the pastor emeritus
status conferred upon Miss Ida Mae Hays by her Brazilian church
upon her return for retirement.'" Upon receiving this e-mail, sitting
in front of my computer, I said out loud, "So what! There are a lot of
things the IMB has not recognized during the years I have been a
missionary. Why should they begin now?"

The first week in February 2002 I received the letter from the
IMB requesting all missionaries to sign the 2000 *Baptist Faith and
Message*. Since I was just three weeks away from officially retiring, I
simply ignored the letter. I had no desire to sign any creed.

On March 1, 2002, I officially retired. There were times when I
was not sure that I would be able to reach retirement. I believe I
came very close to being fired by the IMB. Fortunately, I was finally
invited to Richmond to participate in the retirement recognition in
May. Two weeks after officially retiring I was on a plane returning to
Brazil to make plans and preparations for a Birmingham volunteer
group to return to Brasilia to construct a drug rehabilitation center.

Early in 2003, after only one year into retirement, I began experiencing a restlessness. As I did some soul-searching, I realized that God had permitted my ordination for a reason. I thought, perhaps God was calling me to be a pastor. I finally committed my life again to the Lord to be a pastor, *if* that was the reason for my being ordained. But God would have to take care of the details! Once that decision was made, I had to deal with giving up a comfortable retirement home that had been given to me. I finally gave it up, and God took care of that as well!

I made two trips to Brazil in 2003. In May I traveled to Brasilia to help two Birmingham churches construct a drug rehabilitation center. In July I led a group of women to Brazil to teach at the WMU seminary in Recife. Joy Heaton, the pastor of the Antioch Baptist Church in Enfield, North Carolina, was in that group. One afternoon as we waited in the seminary office to download our e-mail, Joy took a small piece of paper and wrote on it. Then folding the paper, she handed it to me. She had written: "I know a church in North Carolina that would seriously consider you as their pastor. And they have a nice parsonage." God, in his infinite plan for my life, opened wide the door to a retirement ministry that I had prayed for long before I left Brazil. I just did not know that it was to be a pastor. That was not in my plans! I had no idea that this trip would change my life dramatically. God led me back to Brazil to call me to be a pastor.

The next day Joy and I had a brief conversation about the note she had written. I agreed to e-mail my résumé to her upon our return to the United States. Edna Weeks, the chairperson of the Weldon Baptist pastor search committee, received that résumé in less than twenty-four hours. What I did not know was that the day before Joy left to go to Brazil, Mrs. Weeks had called her asking for any recommendations as pastor. Joy did not have anyone to recommend.

Since I was planning to attend the 169th anniversary of Joy's church on August 17, 2003, arrangements were made for an interview with the Weldon pastor search committee that same evening. Five minutes into the interview I knew that God was calling me to the Weldon Baptist Church, and the pastor search committee felt the same thing. I was invited to come and preach on Sunday, September 21. The pastor search committee voted unanimously that day to call me. The next Sunday, September 28, the recommendation was presented to the diaconate, and the vote was unanimous to call me. On Sunday, October 5, the recommendation was taken to the church, and the vote again was unanimous to call me as pastor. I would become the first female pastor at Weldon Baptist Church.

I moved to Weldon, North Carolina, and officially became the pastor of the Weldon Baptist Church on November 16, 2003. On November 23, at the ordination/installation service, the Weldon Baptist Church confirmed my Brazilian ordination, ordained me, and installed me as pastor.

I was told somewhere along the way that the oldest member of the church, Mary Daniel, was 104 years old. Early on, she had communicated with Mrs. Weeks, saying that it was now time for the church to call a woman as pastor. The committee was open to that possibility. It amazes me that Mrs. Mary Daniel, a 104-year old woman, was thinking "outside her generation" and coloring "outside the box"! God does move in miraculous and amazing ways.

I have been pastor of the Weldon Baptist Church for more than a year. I love my church and all its members. I love Weldon, North Carolina. I love the pastoral ministry. The Lord is blessing the work here. Each week, there are new challenges, new goals, and new ministries. The Lord has richly blessed me. I am experiencing more fulfillment and satisfaction as a pastor than I ever experienced in all my years as a missionary.

As I bring my story to a close, I have several observations. I believe the words "courage" and "determination" best describe who I am. I am not a person who runs away from difficulties. I face the conflicts and try to find a solution. Yes, there has been a great deal of opposition to my ordination and to my being a pastor. Some of my dearest friends, missionary colleagues, and family have made unkind remarks and have abandoned any kind of relationship with me. But God has provided a host of others who are supportive and who express their appreciation at every opportune time. I am deeply grateful.

I have no doubt that God called me to be a missionary. Following the command of the Great Commission, Jesus said, "Go ye into all the world and preach the gospel." And I took that as the gospel truth. That command is for everyone: men, women, boys, and girls. Jesus did not say, "Go, you men, into all the world." I, as a woman, found myself in the middle of the Great Commission, hearing the command to "go and preach the gospel." When God calls people, he calls them to "preach the gospel" to everyone and in all places.

So many say that women are not to teach men and be in authority over men. And I am aware that many churches do not permit women to teach boys over twelve years of age and men in Sunday School. Many times in Brazil I found myself witnessing to men because I was the only Christian around to share the gospel. Can you imagine me saying to a man who has inquired about how to be saved: "Well, sir, I really can't tell you about how to be saved because I am a woman, but wait right here, and I will go find a man who can tell you." How absurd! I did not want, nor do I want, the guilt of any man on my hands just because I am told that I cannot preach the gospel because I am a woman.

When I was appointed and commissioned a missionary, my church, the mission board, the denomination, and whoever else had a part in sending me, said to me, "Go and preach the gospel." It was okay for me, as a woman, to witness, to teach, and to preach the gospel to all those "heathens" on the mission field, but when I returned to the States, my homeland, I was told by the same church, the same mission board, and the same denomination that I could not do what I did for thirty-one years of my life in Brazil. What is the difference? I used the same Bible in Brazil that carries the same message as any Bible in the United States.

I have heard over and over the explanations of two or three scripture passages that women are to do such and such and cannot do other things. I cannot, in all honesty, place those two or three scripture passages on one side of the balance, place the whole Bible on the other side of the balance, and make the balance tip in favor of the two or three scripture passages. The overview of the whole Bible outweighs two or three scripture texts.

I have no doubt that God has called me to be a pastor. God has a place of service for me. It was not in "my plans" to be the pastor of a church, but it was in God's plans. All my life, I wanted to be a missionary. But God, not I, flung wide open the doors for me to be a pastor. And I have no choice but to be obedient to the Lord and to follow him.

I still have a great appreciation to the FMB for facilitating my being appointed and fulfilling God's call in my life to serve as a missionary in Brazil and to represent Southern Baptists on the mission field. I have been extremely disappointed in the unfair treatment I received on my return to the United States, after spending the best years of my life as a missionary representing Southern Baptists.

But today I can honestly say I hold no bitterness or anger toward those who have treated me unfairly. Why? Because God has given me the courage and determination to rise above the petty attitudes of those who would "put down" any servant of the Lord just because of her gender. I, as a woman, called of God, can stand tall and firm in my convictions that I have done what God called me to do. God is my judge, not man! I am too blessed to be stressed! When God calls people to ministry, he gives courage enough to follow through on that call.

People who are called by God will most likely have to cope with misunderstandings, conflict, and some bitterness in the course of their ministries, but bitterness cannot be allowed to dominate. There comes a time when, after dealing with conflicts and hurts, a person needs to turn these matters over to the Lord to resolve. God says,

"Vengeance is mine." Leave the matter with the Lord. He can do a much better job in resolving any conflict. When conflicts have come my way and I have had problems dealing with them, I have given them to the Lord and said, "Lord, I can't handle this matter any more. Please take it. I will, in a quiet trust, continue to go about the ministry I know you have called me to do, knowing you are in control of every situation. I know you will resolve the matter in a way that is best for me." The times I have made that kind of commitment to God, he blesses me so much more, and he resolves the conflicts in ways that I never dreamed would be possible.

The writing of this manuscript is a promise and a blessing from God to provide the telling of my story at the appropriate time.

CHAPTER 7

# "When I Am Preaching, I Know in My Bones that I Am Doing What I Was Born To Do"

MARGARET (MEG) B. HESS

It was a dark and stormy night. The weather had been unseasonably cold and wet all month, but on that mid-June night in 1982, the rain was coming down in sheets. Thunder rumbled as lightning lit up the swiftly gathering darkness. Dressed in my oversized black robe, tugging on my new red stole, I jogged from foot to foot at the back of the sanctuary, excitedly whispering to my colleagues as we waited for the service to begin. The occasion was my ordination to Christian ministry by the First Baptist Church in Newton, Massachusetts. I looked down at the worship bulletin held in my hand and reread the quote from T. S. Eliot that I had chosen for the cover: "We shall not cease from exploration/ And the end of all our exploring/ will be to arrive where we started/ and know the place for the first time."[1] I marveled again that the journey had led me to that moment of ordination, an outcome that felt as mysterious as it did right. As the organ began to play the opening hymn, I found myself dancing down the aisle, borne up by the awareness that love moves in mysterious ways.

My journey to ordination began long before I knew where I was headed. My earliest childhood memories were of church. As a toddler I remember being in the church nursery, standing on my tiptoes to look over the top of the half door as the church ladies came to cluck and coo over the babies. Later, when I was old enough to sit through worship, I would rub my fingers over the deep mahogany velvet of the cushions while staring up at the stained glass window of Jesus cradling a sheep in his arms. As the preacher droned on, I would color in the clouds on the drawing of the church on the bulletin cover. Kicking my feet back and forth, I wiggled and squirmed until my sister poked me in the ribs or my parents gave me "The Look," at which time I would start examining the other stained glass window of Jesus agonizing in the garden of Gethsemane.

The good people of the First Baptist Church of Danville, Virginia, took seriously their commitment to educate me in the faith, which they had made when I was dedicated as an infant. Mae Harley helped me to memorize Bible verses that had been typed on tiny strips of paper, then rolled up and stuffed into pill casings. She challenged us to take our "Bible verse vitamins" seriously, which I did. Harrison Gregory told the story of Joseph and his coat of many colors so vividly that I still can hear the forlorn Joseph calling out in vain from the bottom of the pit where his brothers had left him until they could sell him off to the highest bidder. Luke Smith plunged me into the waters of baptism, initiating me into the priesthood of all believers. After I answered her questions about Bible stories correctly, Mary Lou Barr proclaimed proudly, "You can tell your mother you passed with flying colors," as she approved my move to the next level of Girls' Auxiliary (GA). And Sunday after Sunday, year after year, Sally Soyers taught me about abiding presence when she said to me, "I've *still* got that seashell you brought me," referring to a small shell I had given her after a trip to the beach when I was five. I was surrounded by so great a cloud of witnesses.

Though First Baptist's theological posture was what I would describe as "moderate," I was still heavily influenced by the religious atmosphere of the South; it was a part of the air that I breathed. Unusual, "Christ-haunted" characters dotted the landscape of southern Virginia. An old woman stood on a downtown corner handing out tracts to anyone in her range. A man with wild hair and a ragged beard walked around town dressed in a burlap sack, shaking a walking stick and shouting, "Repent." Revival preachers told stories of young people who died tragically before they could accept Jesus as their personal Savior. The tracts that everyone seemed to have stuffed into their zippered Bibles told of the horrors that awaited the unsaved as the "end times" came upon us. Books like *The Late Great Planet Earth* made my blood run cold with its end times prophecies. Being a nervous child to start with, these theologies of Christian terrorism made me wring my hands in the dark of night.

In my teen years, caught up in the "Jesus movement," I attended every revival service and prayer meeting I could. At the end of the services, "with every head bowed and every eye closed," I found myself propelled to the altar as I responded to the invitation to follow Christ again and again. When all was said and done, I had been saved more times than beef stew.

By the time I went off to college I was ripe for some good theological education. Fortunately, I found a patient guide in Dr. Roger Crook, chair of the religion department at Meredith College in Raleigh, North Carolina, where I was a student. Under his tutelage, I began to study scripture, ethics, theology, and church history. In the academic study of religion I felt as if a whole new world was opening up to me. Something began to shift in my relationship with God. My faith was less anxiety driven and more characterized by trust. Faith became less about "being saved" and more about figuring out how to align myself with God's just and compassionate activity in the world. I decided to add religion as my second major, as I was hungry for more knowledge.

As I neared the completion of my undergraduate study at Meredith, I started puzzling about "what next." I had followed Dr. Crook's advice to study what I loved, but I was not certain that a double major in American history and religion had prepared me for the job market. I spent hours talking with Dr. Crook and the campus chaplain, Larry Williams, another kindhearted guide, about my career choices. With their encouragement, I decided to apply to seminary. Given that the academic study of religion had freed me in so many ways and deepened my faith in Christ, I felt strongly drawn to teaching. I figured that acquiring a Master of Divinity degree would give me a broad base of study, and from that I could pursue doctoral studies. My call to ministry was beginning to take shape, and it went something like this: "I want to do for others what Dr. Crook has done for me." Dr. Crook had taught me to think for myself, and that gift had drawn me closer to God. I imagined myself a college professor like him. Pastoral ministry never occurred to me.

As I explored my options for seminary, I decided not to attend a Southern Baptist seminary. Having been educated at a Southern Baptist women's college and having traveled in narrow Southern Baptist religious circles, I felt that I would benefit from being challenged by other perspectives. I chose to attend Andover Newton Theological School in Newton Centre, Massachusetts, because it was in a different part of the country and because it was a part of the Boston Theological Institute (BTI), a consortium of theological schools that provided the opportunity to cross register amongst the schools. Having access to the BTI would give me a broad base of study and more choices for postgraduate work, I reasoned.

During my first year of seminary, I began work at the First Baptist Church in Malden, Massachusetts, in order to meet my field education requirement. A multi-staffed church with three seminarian members left little opportunity for the student ministers to participate in leading worship. It was months into the job before I had an opportunity to take a small role in worship leadership.

My big moment came when I was invited to lead the pastoral prayer for the day. I had a great deal of anxiety about public speaking, especially in the worship context. Giving the task my best efforts, I prayed an earnest and heart-felt prayer. After the service, a choir member came up to me. Dr. Houghton had been professor of worship at Boston University School of Theology years before. "Have you taken a course in how to deliver pastoral prayers?" he asked. "No," I replied. "Then you need to," he said, and walked off. I was devastated by the criticism and vowed never to get "up front" again.

In 1979, the summer after my first year in seminary, I returned to my home church for a visit. The pastor had recently left his post there, so I met with the associate pastor, Richard Peery. I told him that after working in a church for a year I was beginning to think that I had gifts for pastoral ministry, though I was still hesitant about worship leadership. When he heard that I was thinking of pastoral ministry, he laughed. He was not being unkind, rather he was being honest about how difficult it would be for a woman to pursue ministry in the Southern Baptist Convention (SBC) at that time. Stubborn as I was, I took this as a personal challenge. That was about the same time I began to have dreams about preaching.

The dream that haunted me the most was this: I was to preach in my home church in Danville. I got up to preach, but I had no notes, no manuscript, nor did I even know on which biblical text I was supposed to preach. I was terrified. I looked out at the congregation, which was predominantly male. They looked back at me with disapproval. Then I looked at a man who was sitting on the front row, the man who had just introduced me to the congregation. In waking life the man was L. D. Johnson, a prominent Southern Baptist clergyman who had been the pastor of my home church when I was a child. In the dream Dr. Johnson had an eager look on his face. He leaned forward in anticipation. Everything about his body language said to me, "Go ahead Meg, you have something to say." I woke in a cold sweat, panicked by the possibility of preaching.

In waking life I trusted Dr. Johnson's wisdom, having read his newspaper columns for years. In my dream he was a larger than life figure. As the primary figure of the dream, I felt he was trying to tell me something. Why should I not listen to him? After all, he was the person who had dedicated me to God when I was an infant.

I puzzled over what the dream might be telling me. In the biblical tradition God spoke through dreams and people's lives were changed by those dreams. As I was discussing the dream with a friend, he focused on the part of the dream that made me anxious: I did not have a sermon and I did not know what to do about it. "Maybe the dream is just telling you to write a sermon," he suggested. His interpretation seemed reasonable, I thought, so I signed up for a preaching course.

While taking a preaching class taught by Eddie S. O'Neal, I discovered that I loved to preach. Something happened to me when I preached that I can only describe as a mystical experience. I felt connected to God in a deep and transforming way. Preaching challenged and changed me, from the preparation process through the delivery. This passion for preaching came as a surprise to me; it was not a part of my plan.

The summer after my preaching class, I was invited to preach at the First Baptist Church in Danville. Bob Forehand was the interim pastor at the time, and I will be forever grateful to him for instigating that invitation. In sharing the pulpit with me, he was willing to take a risk in order to support a daughter of the church.

When a deacon called to extend the invitation to preach, he said, "We would like to ask you to speak at our morning worship service." "Let me be clear," I said. "Do you want me to *speak* or to *preach*?" "Well," he hesitated, "we'd like for you to preach." I said yes.

Up to that point, I had almost no women models for doing this kind of ministry. There had been strong women leaders in the Danville church, but none that I knew of were ordained. Women had not begun to serve as deacons in that church until the early 1970s, less than ten years before. Women who spoke publicly did so primarily in the context of Southern Baptist missions. When attending Camp Viewmont, a GA camp outside of Charlottesville,

Virginia, I had heard stories of Lottie Moon and other strong women missionaries, but the stories did not focus on their preaching abilities.

While in college I had often attended worship at Duke University, where a woman on staff there participated in leading worship. I found her unexpected voice to be annoying, I was so used to the booming male preacher. One of my instructors in the practice preaching class, Jamie Howard, had been a United Church of Christ pastor for years, but I had never heard her preach. I felt at sea as I entered the uncharted waters of women's preaching. I was not sure what my preaching voice would, or should, sound like.

My sermon in Danville was my first during a morning worship service. I was so nervous that I thought I would fall over in a dead faint. As I sat up front, I kept remembering the dream I had the year before. The thought of an encouraging Dr. Johnson sitting there calmed my nerves enough so that I could get through my sermon. I preached for all I was worth, giving it my best effort. Would this congregation support or deny my growing call to ministry? Sally Soyers sat perched on the fifth row, frail and old, fragile as a bone china tea cup. After the service, she slipped her paper thin hand into mine and whispered in the voice of old age, "I am so proud of my girl. I've still got that sea shell you gave me." I was on my way to ordination, blessed by the cloud of witnesses.

Also present in worship that day was Richard, the pastor with whom I had met the previous year. He had left First Baptist Church, Danville, for another post, but happened to be back visiting that Sunday. After the service, he said to me, "God will have a place for you to preach."

Midway through seminary, I made the decision to move my membership into the American Baptist Churches, USA, and joined the First Baptist Church in Newton, Massachusetts, where I was a field education student. As my emerging call moved me more in the direction of preaching, it became clear that pastoral ministry would be difficult for me in the SBC. I felt as if I had to choose my battles carefully. Years later, Dr. Crook would remind me that at one time he had expressed hope that I would remain with the SBC. "We need pioneers," he had said. "I don't want to be a pioneer," I replied. "I want to be a pastor."

Preaching had become such a passion for me that the decision to be ordained to that function seemed like a natural progression. I have always held what I term a "low church" view of ordination. I take seriously the priesthood of all believers and think that when the church ordains one to a particular function it is more about accountability than about someone being special or superior. God gave me gifts for preaching and I wished to use them in a faithful way to encourage the growth and development of God's people. I went through the usual pedestrian struggles that one has when called to preach: resisting, lamenting my unworthiness, and feeling like I was not equal to the task. I suspect that anytime God invites us to grow beyond our present abilities we all go through a similar struggle. For what is "call" but God's gracious invitation to move more deeply into the mystery of being transformed by the mind of Christ Jesus? My call just happened to involve entering into a profession that did not always embrace women.

I have never felt fully at home as a pastor. Paradoxically, when I am preaching, I know in my bones that I am doing what I was born to do. I have not felt at home for many reasons, the most obvious being that I am a woman in a profession with few women role models. Also, I am as prone to doubt as I am to faith. When the scales tip too far in the direction of doubt, then preaching becomes more difficult than usual. My first sermon in Danville was on the text of Jacob wrestling with God on a river in the dark of night. The metaphor of wrestling with God has suited my ministry from the beginning.

My ordination process was a joyful one, and I received a lot of support from the members of First Baptist, Newton, and others in their American Baptist association. Fortunately, those present at my ordination council were mostly encouraging. The one objection to my qualifications came from a pastor who strongly believed that all pastors should have studied Greek and Hebrew, which I had not. That debate aside, my emergent internal call to pastoral ministry was affirmed by those gathered. Internal authority was mirrored by the conferred authority of the church.

At the time, my ordination seemed to be the completion of a long process of discerning my vocation. In retrospect, I see that it was one marker in a lifelong journey of clarifying what it means to be a baptized Christian, baptism being the moment when all Christians enter into their call to ministry. My understandings of call and faithfulness have continued to evolve throughout my pastoral ministry. My sense of voice as a woman preacher is ever deepening.

At my ordination, Norm De Puy, the new pastor at First Baptist, Newton, began his charge to the congregation by saying, "Jesus was assassinated by his congregation." I was pastoring my first church at the time and they all laughed as Norm then asked the members of that church to identify themselves. His words eerily foreshadowed the conflicted ending I would have at that church. About five and a half years into my ministry there, a faulty wiring problem would start a fire in the middle of the night that destroyed the church building. Seminary had not prepared me to deal with such a crisis. After a year-and-a-half building project, we dedicated the new church facility. Shortly after, I left in the middle of a conflict. My lack of experience, errors in judgment, and immaturity combined to leave me caught in a power struggle I did not survive. The trauma of the fire moved us into a regressive, reactive state that affected the functioning of the church in ways that none of us fully understood at the time. That ending was a wound that will always pain me. At the time, it moved me into a reexamination of my call.

Completely burned out emotionally and wondering if I should leave pastoral ministry altogether, I accepted a call to be the interim minister at the Old Cambridge Baptist Church (OCBC) in Cambridge, Massachusetts. There I began to heal, to recover my love of preaching, and to move more fully into a sense of my authenticity as a preacher. At OCBC the pastor preached twice a month and lay people preached the other Sundays. Listening to so many gifted lay preachers taught me that each person has a sermon and that my job was to cultivate *my* unique voice for *my* sermon.

While at OCBC, I began my Doctor of Ministry degree in pastoral counseling at Andover Newton. My doctoral work with Earl Thompson and Brita Gill-Austern introduced me to family systems theory, which gave me new skills for healthier functioning as a pastor. That work moved me further into my healing, for I used my training to be a therapist as a way to explore my own unresolved family of origin issues and how they affected my pastoral leadership. I wrote my doctoral thesis on women and preaching, deepening my sense of who I was as a female preacher.[2]

After a second interim in Plymouth, Massachusetts, I accepted the call to become the pastor of the First Baptist Church in Nashua, New Hampshire, where I served for nine rich years. During that time, in addition to my pastoral work, I developed a small pastoral psychotherapy practice where I continued the work of proclaiming a liberating word; it was just in a smaller setting than the pulpit.

In 1983, when I was two years out of seminary, Eddie O'Neal invited me to join the team that taught the practice preaching class at Andover Newton. I taught with him until his retirement in 2000. Since then, I have designed and taught an introductory preaching course called Holistic Preaching. In that course I not only teach the basics of sermon construction, but I also explore with the students the things that block or enhance the development of our voice as preachers. My own journey informs my desire to support others to develop their authentic voice for preaching.

The labyrinthine journey of ministry has led me into some interesting places: some painful, some joyful, all deeply enriching. In 2002, twenty-one years after my ordination there, I returned to the First Baptist Church in Newton, Massachusetts, as the interim pastor. In so many ways, I felt like I was coming full circle. I had left there as a student minister in 1981, full of optimism and enthusiasm. I returned as a seasoned pastor with a few battle scars, a deeper sense of my identity, and a heightened taste of God's gracious, redeeming presence in my life. In my first sermon there as interim, I recalled Eliot's words from *Four Quartets*: "With the drawing of this love, and the voice of this calling, we shall not cease from exploration."[3] I felt as if I was addressing my former self, reminding me that my ministry journey will always be one of exploration lived out in relationship with a loving God.

As I write this article my full-time job is parenting our daughter, Keziah, whom my husband, Peter Lacey, and I adopted from China in 2001. I continue to have a small pastoral psychotherapy practice, to teach preaching at Andover Newton, to write, and to preach every chance I get. Preaching for all of these years has been a gift and a privilege. Preaching is an organic event in which my encounter with the biblical text takes root in me and changes me in ever surprising ways. I think with gratitude of the women ministers, both lay and ordained, who have gone before me, and of all of my mentors who have supported my growth in ministry along the way. I think with hope of the women who will read this. I pray that you will trust God's calling in your life and that with the "drawing" of that love and with the "voice" of that calling, you will move forward into ministry with courage and hope.

# CHAPTER 8

# "Let's Explore the Possibilities": The Story of Alma Hunt

## CATHERINE B. ALLEN

"Plenipotentiary" describes one who has highest authority to take independent action. Plenipotentiary describes Alma Hunt, minister of the gospel, missionary, and mentor.[1] She is not ordained and has declined the opportunity to be ordained. She was never encouraged to preach. She never felt a particular calling for ministry. Yet Alma believes in all of the above and practices all of the above. Few people have preached as much, in as many countries, with such obvious anointing of the Holy Spirit, and with such passionate principles as this devoted apostle.

Alma is a law unto herself and a legend in her own time. She has been called "the mother of missions" for Southern Baptists. Nowadays, she prefers to be identified as a Virginia Baptist or a Baptist World Alliance member. She is a transitional figure from the day when a woman's only professional opportunity was to teach school, to this current era in which a woman can be a pulpit preacher, a theology professor, or a pastor.

In ninety-five years of her life thus far, Alma has lived with a sense of adventuring with God. When confronted by controversy or creativity she always says, "Let's explore the possibilities." She keeps the door open for God to reveal something new and exciting every day. Her optimism is amazing considering the cruel twists of history she has seen. She has her flashes of anger, and her sharp wit can unleash a sharper tongue. Yet she has found a more excellent way: to lead boldly on principle in order to make a way for women and men to become all that God has intended.

Missions was the only Christian professional work open to women in Alma's earliest years. Most women missionaries were teachers. Baptists had been willing to appoint women as foreign missionaries for less than fifty years when she began "exploring the possibilities" for her own life. By the time she was middle-aged, two-thirds of Baptist foreign missionaries were women. But after Alma's first retirement in 1974, the percentage of female missionaries steadily declined. That decline may be attributed to the Southern Baptist Convention's (SBC) ban of women from pastoral ministries and its severe restriction of women from any form of service that involved leadership, except among other women. Despite the decline of female missionaries and the ban on women's leadership, several Baptist women during the 1970s were being ordained, and several ordained women were serving as missionaries. An examination of the life and attitudes of Alma provides some understanding of the rise and collapse of Southern Baptist women in ministry.

Alma broke traditions, forged new possibilities for women in ministry, and mentored thousands of women and men. When she saw her labors for the rights and recognition of women in ministry denounced by the SBC, she instituted new ways in which women could serve, and at the age of ninety-five, she is still exploring possibilities for people to proclaim Christ through word and deed.

Born October 9, 1909, in Roanoke, Virginia, Alma was reared in the nurture and admonition of the Lord, as interpreted by the First Baptist Church of Roanoke and her church-going parents. Her childhood pastor was John Vines, whose wife Valeria was the state president of the Baptist Woman's Missionary Union (WMU) and a formidable leader. When Alma was about nine years old, she was elected president of her church's Girls' Auxiliary (GAs). At her first meeting, she fumbled through her duties. Mrs. Vines said, "Alma, you are making a mess of things. Now sit down, and stand up and try again." With the strict guidance of Vines and others in the church, Alma mastered all the standard formats of leadership.

Alma's primary skills for public leadership were inborn. She made and kept hundreds of friends. She was full of zest and enthusiasm for life. Alma created fun, had big dreams, and enticed people to help her achieve them. To these inborn skills, she added learned skills in organization, loyalty, and dutiful discipline.

Women were exceptionally visible as leaders in Alma's church. The first professional church musician in the region was Eula Transeau Ligon, the choir director of Alma's church and her close friend. Ligon was the first woman in the South to graduate from Westminster Choir College. Her professionalism made a big impression on several pastors and sparked their interest in forming a school of church music. Eventually, these pastors and others formed that school at Southern Baptist Theological Seminary. Yet not many women had the opportunity in the early twentieth century to serve churches as choir directors or music leaders because as the salaries for these positions increased, church music became a man's job.

As she began contemplating her future, Alma knew that if she could not find a church music position, she could become a missionary or she could seek employment with the WMU and its growing network of employed promoters. The WMU in those days offered a well-defined and well-protected channel for women to serve as leaders. Thousands of women served in voluntary capacities and some gave all their time and resources to the WMU. Women employed by the WMU made a meager but adequate living.

Alma had numerous friends serving as missionaries and as WMU employees, and she avidly supported and encouraged them, but she did not intend to follow them into any of these professions, for she had decided to be a schoolteacher. Alma did, however, agree to serve as a volunteer in the WMU organization, and in that capacity she worked her way from local to regional leadership in the

WMU's programs for girls, which she enjoyed. The next step for her was to move into statewide and national leadership. After one session at the national young women's camp held at Ridgecrest Baptist Assembly grounds in North Carolina, she was asked to lead recreation at subsequent annual camps, a perfect volunteer summer job for Alma.

Around 1927 Alma began to study at the State Teachers College (now Longwood University), a woman's college in Farmville, Virginia. On her first trip home, she demonstrated what she had learned: how to stand on her head and do flips. When her family experienced financial difficulties, Alma was forced to leave college and find a job. She was qualified to teach primary school, so in 1929 she took a teaching position at Clearbrook School, located in a remote, rural corner of Roanoke County.

At the age of nineteen, Alma met her first class, fifty-eight children in the third and fourth grades. They were sitting in double desks bolted to the floor. Because of limited transportation to her rural school, she often had to spend the night in the homes of her students. Alma taught for two years, and in 1931, at the age of twenty-one, she was appointed principal of the Clearbrook School. Later, she taught elementary school in Roanoke and helped to found the Grandin Court School also in Roanoke. Alma was a much-loved and effective teacher, and even after she had turned ninety years old, her former students continued to seek her out. One elderly woman testified in 2004: "She was the best teacher I ever had. Everybody loved her. We were not afraid of her. So we learned more."

During summers, Alma found lucrative and delightful employment directing camps in the northeast. She also took summer courses and eventually earned her bachelor's degree in education. Alma loved her life as a teacher and a school principal. Yet she continued throughout her early adulthood to be involved in volunteer work for the WMU.

Asked about this period of her life, Alma denies that she had a calling from God. She was not thinking in those terms. She did have a commitment to serve God and to have as much fun as possible. Gradually, she came to believe that missions was the most important work a person could do, and she became convinced that women's involvement in missions was an essential way for the gospel to be spread—especially to women in other cultures.

Among Alma's best friends during these years was a woman she met through the WMU, Ida Paterson Storm. Storm first served as a Baptist missionary in China and then married, changed denominations, and served in the Middle East among Muslims. Alma observed that Storm and other women like her were winning both men and women to Christ, and so unlike many of her day, Alma believed that women missionaries could and should be influential in evangelism among both genders.

Even if God did not call Alma, the WMU did call her and kept calling her. She received regular letters from Ethlene Cox, the treasurer and the former national president of the WMU, who addressed her as "Dear Winsome Elf." Juliette Mather, the noted young people's leader for the WMU, urged Alma to leave her school teaching and enroll in the WMU Training School. Mather wanted Alma to have the highest credentials available to women of the time for Christian service.

The WMU Training School was a powerful influence in the Southern Baptist denomination. The school was the first and most welcoming place in which Southern Baptist women could obtain theological training. The Training School produced skilled and disciplined graduates who constantly pushed the limits of what women traditionally had done in public ministry. Yet the graduates showed the polished graces and restraint that usually made them acceptable within Baptist circles. The WMU Training School virtually guaranteed a young woman professional employment in ministry. A larger number of female Southern Baptist missionaries were produced by this school than by any other.

Because the WMU gave and controlled much mission money, the SBC mission boards appointed women missionaries to do ministries that the WMU favored, usually related to the needs of women and children. Many of the Training School graduates found positions in social work institutions owned and operated at the time by the WMU system. Other graduates joined church staffs as secretaries and religious education directors, positions that were then considered appropriate for women. Even with all its achievements, or maybe because of them, the WMU Training School was ridiculed by many pastors and denominational leaders. The school was feared as much as it was appreciated.

Despite the encouragement of Mather, Alma did not enroll as a student at the WMU Training School. Instead, she became close friends with many of the school's graduates and acquired from them some of their learning and skills. These peers were influential in her life. The other determining human influence on Alma's young adult years was her pastor in Roanoke, Walter Pope Binns, who was perhaps best known for his promotion of Baptist principles related to the separation of church and state. Both he and his wife gave special support to Alma during her years of blossoming leadership. They and the church provided her with anything she needed as she staged meetings and mission projects and as she entertained important leaders. In her later years, Alma said of Binns, "He molded me. He wanted me to reach higher than I thought possible. He wanted me to be myself, not to imitate others."

Binns warned her against becoming a clone of the WMU system of the day. He believed that the denomination had room for women to serve beyond the WMU. Yet he also affirmed the WMU network—as long as it allowed the true Alma to shine through.

When Alma was invited to make her first formal speech to a national WMU audience, Binns and his wife polished her for the opportunity. He instructed her to avoid the speaking mannerisms popular among the WMU trainees. He believed that Alma's natural voice and charming delivery were superior. His wife helped Alma select her clothes, assisted with the final grooming, and reminded her, "Do all your grooming in the privacy of your room. When you are on stage, do not touch your hair, your dress, or your face. Keep both feet solidly on the floor. You look fine, so forget yourself. Concentrate on your audience." Mrs. Binns then sat attentively while Alma wrote and practiced her speech. By being herself, but keenly mindful of making a good impression, Alma surpassed the standards of both men and women arbiters of women's roles.

Despite Alma's reluctance to attend the WMU Training School, Juliette Mather did not give up on her young friend. Mather's commitment to encourage young women to follow God's calling and to prepare for service resulted in her writing letters to Alma for thirteen and one-half years. Her notes arrived at strategic times in a year: moments of decision, challenge, or crisis. Mather was still praying for Alma to attend the Training School, perhaps to become the youth leader for a state WMU office. But Alma still had received no special calling from God. She was enjoying life, going happily through interesting doors as they opened.

When Binns became president of William Jewell College, a Baptist school in Liberty, Missouri, he invited Alma to become dean of women for the college. She realized for the first time that her role as an educator could be a Christian ministry. Advanced education was now essential for her. During summers, she earned a master's degree and did further studies at Columbia University in New York. Her specialty was a relatively new field of student personnel service, involving counseling and management. Delighted with her new profession and her studies, she still maintained her high interest in missions as an avocation.

Missouri WMU leaders who watched her success in college administration were also pondering the future of the WMU. Among them were key women who successfully challenged the prevailing image and programs of the WMU. Even though their efforts were initially squelched, the reformers ultimately won when they selected Alma to be the chief executive officer for the national WMU.

Alma, with her lipstick, fingernail polish, shorts, athletic ability, and secular master's degree, provided a shocking freshness for the

WMU. When she walked into the WMU office in Birmingham, Alabama, in 1948, she greeted Mather by saying, "Be careful what you pray for, Miss Mather. Here I am."

During her twenty-six years at the helm of the WMU, membership of the organization reached its peak of 1.5 million members who were organized for mission support in more than 75 percent of Southern Baptist churches. Of those members, about half were boys and girls. The WMU system constantly reminded those children of God's call to mission service.

Alma was now the only female in the ranks of SBC leadership. Yet the majority of male denominational leaders were products of WMU training in childhood. Many of the younger men had begun their professional careers as employees of the WMU's missions education system. The atmosphere in which the lone woman leader worked was filled with mutual appreciation, admiration, and good humor. She was also fearless in argument and honest expression of her opinions. Some people praised her by saying, "Alma has the mind of a man. Look at how the men listen to her." One of her WMU board members commented in 1974, "Alma has the mind of a good woman."

In keeping with her own authenticity, Alma made it a point to be feminine and fashionable. She was stylishly slim, kept her fingernails perfectly manicured with red polish, and wore her blonde hair curled. Being a woman was a strength for her, not a liability. Her style worked with female audiences and male audiences alike.

The years of her service as leader of the national WMU saw much change. One change may be noted by examining her speaking schedule. Until about 1964 she was in much demand as a speaker at weekday women's mission meetings. For the last forty years, she has been in demand to "bring the message" and even to preach from Sunday morning pulpits.

Administratively, Alma juggled many changes. During her watch, the WMU relinquished ownership of the WMU Training School. The school could not gain accreditation as it was structured, and many Baptists felt that women might be able to secure ministry positions if they had the same theological education experience as men had. The church positions that had once been deemed to belong to women, such as religious education, music, and campus ministry, were now being taken on by seminary-educated men. Yet even after the Training School closed and the percentage of women enrolled in Southern Baptist seminaries increased, women found it increasingly difficult to obtain jobs in ministry.

As the WMU executive director, Alma formed numerous harmonious and collegial relationships. Her closest working partner was Marie Mathis, the voluntary president of the WMU for thirteen years and a member of the WMU staff for six years. In 1963 Mathis was elected second-vice-president of the SBC, the first woman to achieve such a post. From that date, the WMU leaders were steadily crossing over into formerly male bastions, serving as trustees, state convention presidents, and SBC officers. These WMU leaders opened the way for the elections of women who had not been particularly active in the WMU.

In addition to her work as leader of the WMU, Alma was a decisive participant in the development of the Women's Department of the Baptist World Alliance (BWA), especially its North American component. In 1970 she became a vice-president of the BWA. As vice president, she was asked to preside over a session at the 1975 BWA Congress, making her the first woman ever to preside at a meeting of this organization. Alma cultivated a peer group of decisive women leaders in several other countries. She corresponded avidly with her "far-flung friends."

In the 1960s, during the rocky civil rights movement in the United States, as violence erupted outside her Birmingham office, Alma gave the WMU a progressive voice. During that same time frame, an off-shoot of the civil rights movement, the women's liberation movement, hit the WMU and Alma with a significant challenge. Many WMU members swapped their full-time voluntary church work for the paying job market. The WMU enrollment and literature sales declined. Prior to her retirement, Alma led a major overhaul of the WMU so that the organization could appeal to this new kind of Baptist woman, but the denomination as a whole did not echo her progressive message, and a conservative backlash begin to hit the WMU.

The women's liberation movement also brought other unanticipated consequences to the Southern Baptist world. In the mid-1970s Alma first heard women say that they were called to a pastoral ministry. Many of these women had heard the call of God while participating in the WMU studies. With characteristic honesty, the WMU leader met the coming era with optimism and openness. Alma never interfered with a person's effort to follow God's call, and neither did the WMU under her leadership or during the leadership of her immediate successor, Carolyn Weatherford (later Crumpler). Both women were vocal in public in support of women following God's call without limits. They considered the progress of women into pastoral roles a natural outgrowth of all they had been teaching for years. They believed women had always done more than their culture permitted in order to accomplish the work of God.

In 1974 Alma celebrated her sixty-fifth birthday and retired from the national WMU. Soon after her retirement, Aline Fuselier, a member of the WMU staff in Birmingham, was ordained as a deacon. Fuselier then announced her sense of God's calling into a pastoral ministry, and she was actively encouraged by the new chief executive of the WMU, Carolyn Weatherford. Fuselier resigned from her WMU position in 1977, entered training for pastoral counseling, and was ordained for ministry by the Baptist Church of the Covenant in 1978, making her the first-known Baptist woman in Birmingham ordained for ministry.[2]

In 1978 Alma moved to Richmond, Virginia. She joined the staff of the SBC Foreign Mission Board (FMB) as an unpaid worldwide consultant in women's work and traveled to nearly 100 countries to assist missionaries and national leaders in training women for leadership and service. Alma observed firsthand the power of women as leaders of the house-church movements. She attended churches whose members were almost 100 percent female. She talked with women who had heard the call of God and found that women in other cultures sometimes heard God's voice more clearly than did women from her own culture.

Alma continued this international service until 1988. During those ten years of her work with the FMB, the board appointed several ordained women as missionaries and several of them served in pastoral capacities. Development of women's leadership seemed to be a hallmark of the board's mission strategy.

In 1998 Alma retired from her position as a volunteer consultant, and following this second retirement, she returned to her native city of Roanoke. The WMU of Virginia and the Baptist General Association of Virginia named their state missions offering for her, and soon that offering grew to support missions around the world.

In 1995 the SBC celebrated its 150th anniversary with a brief salute to the past, and Alma was one of five historic leaders invited to address the convention. She received a standing ovation. In her speech, she said that missions was the cause that made her get up in the morning and continue to serve, and she pled with the convention to keep its focus on missions. She was the last woman to stand before the convention and speak the truth without compromise. Her significance was not just in her words, but in who she was and what she symbolized for missions and for women. At least some people present recognized her as a symbol of hope.

By 1995, however, the convention had begun calling a halt to its affirmation of women in leadership and ministry. In that same convention session that applauded Alma, messengers voted for a reorganization plan that stripped the WMU of its status as the premier promoter of missions, and its leaders felt forced to accept the plan in public.

A limited status for women was voted into doctrine by the SBC in 1998; and in 2000 women were denied the possibility of pastoral ministry in SBC churches. In early 2003 Alma's own beloved church in Roanoke took a hard line in support of the SBC's anti-woman stance. The church also withdrew from the Baptist General Association of Virginia. For her church and its new pastor to take such an action can only be viewed as a deliberate slap in the face of its own ninety-three-year-old daughter, who was then desperately sick following hospitalization. Yet hundreds of people in that church dearly loved her, continued to involve her in their activities, and seemed oblivious to the significance of their support for the SBC. They even contributed to the Alma Hunt Offering for Virginia Missions, even though their church did not support Virginia missions. It was a harsh and complicated picture of what was happening to all women in the SBC. What could women do under such circumstances?

Alma's decision was to move on, carrying with her the good things of the past and forgetting the bad. Within a week, she moved her membership to Rosalind Hills Baptist Church, which was affiliated with the Cooperative Baptist Fellowship and the Baptist General Association of Virginia. From its beginning, Alma showed up to support the Cooperative Baptist Fellowship. One of its precepts from its beginning in 1991 was the equality of women and men.

In 2001 Alma stepped forward as one of the incorporators of Global Women, a new woman-to-woman missions movement that affirms women in unlimited options for ministry and missions. She remains steadfast in her promotion of the historic principles of the WMU and enthusiastically encourages the creative new and fully egalitarian ministries of the WMU of Virginia.

At least six women have recently invited Alma to participate in their ordination. Some are Baptists, some are former Baptists, and some are former members of her old church in Roanoke. She also took great pleasure in helping with the installation service of Sarah Jackson Shelton as pastor of the Baptist Church of the Covenant in Birmingham. Sarah is the daughter of Alma's former pastor, Lamar Jackson. Alma helped to nurture Sarah from birth to the pulpit, and she championed Sarah's calling in the 1980s, even when Sarah's father needed some convincing.

In 2004 Alma was elated with plans for the ordination of Dr. Alice W. Hunt, who is one of thousands of SBC missionary children who have been under Alma's influence. (Dr. Hunt is not related to Alma.) Dr. Hunt is associate dean of academic affairs at Vanderbilt University Divinity School in Nashville, Tennessee. The following is quoted from a letter Dr. Hunt wrote to her "Aunt Alma," a title customarily used within the missionary network:

> Maybe you remember the Sunday when you preached at First Baptist Church of Boaz. That was the day that it crystallized for me that God was calling me to a particular ministry. If I had been male, I would have recognized more clearly that God was calling me to ordained ministry. But our institutional system was [and still is] living in sin and, because I trusted in that system more than I trusted in God's call to me, I assumed God was calling me to something else. Lest you think that was a negative experience, let me assure you that it was not. I clearly remember giving myself that day to whatever God wanted of me. Because I continued on a path, accentuated particularly that day, to seek after God with all my heart, today I am preparing myself for ordination.[3]

Dr. Hunt's family is among the hundreds of families who maintain devoted friendships with Alma. These relationships are one of the more pleasant and productive legacies from the years of Alma's official leadership in the SBC. But because a generation of SBC leaders arose that rejected Alma's principles, a brilliant theologian like Alice Hunt is now serving a non-Baptist seminary and will be ordained in a Baptist church that developed outside of the SBC.

To embrace and encompass new possibilities, Alma has had to continue growing through her long life. One of her personal stretching points came in 1964, when she was fifty-five years old. That year, Mildred McMurry, one of her dearest friends, died. McMurry had served under Alma as an employee of the WMU, yet she was a giant to whom Alma looked for guidance. Many recall

McMurry as one of the most controversial and powerful preachers
and writers during the civil rights era. Alma had hired her, traveled in
many lands with her, nursed her, fed her, and comforted her in death.
But Alma was unnerved when Earl Stallings, McMurry's pastor at
First Baptist Church of Birmingham, wanted her to be the primary
speaker at her dear friend's funeral.[4] Alma had never seen a woman
speak at a funeral. Women occasionally spoke at memorial services
attended mainly by women, but women never spoke at funerals, and
this funeral would be attended by hundreds of people including civic
leaders of both races. Yet Alma knew that Stallings was right. It was
time for a woman to preach a funeral, and there were no better
persons for whom to break tradition than Mildred McMurry and Earl
Stallings. Alma conquered her own grief, exhaustion, and fear of
criticism in order to do it. She was a historic woman speaking at a
historic moment for a historic woman and church.

Funerals, festivals, weddings, communion services, ordinations,
revivals, banquets, talent shows, panoramic pageants, all-night
committee meetings, boring statistical reports, rousing rallies—Alma
has led them all. And isn't she a woman? Yet she declined when one
of her preferred churches asked for the privilege of giving her formal
ordination. The church told her, "It would encourage other women."
Alma replied, "I'm encouraging women every day." She asked,
"What would ordination have allowed me to do that I have not
already done? Ordination is not the most important thing. Seeking
and serving God is important."

As excellent a public leader as she has been, Alma is perhaps
most excellent in private counseling. The highest privilege, she
believes, is helping another person to find the joy of following and
serving the Lord Jesus. How does she do this? "There is not any one
pattern for this process," she says. "Each person is a unique creation
of God." Alma advises Christian leaders to loosen up and allow
people to be themselves. She also advises counselors and would-be
ministers to make themselves likeable. She thinks ministers should
surround themselves with young people and children as much as

possible. About her own techniques in relating to others, she says, "I try to see each one as an individual. I listen and give the person an opportunity to ask questions. It is important for a person to hear her own voice exploring the possibilities. My job is to help a person recognize what God might help him or her to do." Alma offers these suggestions for people who are seeking God's leadership:

Pray. Believe that God hears prayers and answers prayers. Recognize the answer.

Find several persons you respect. Talk about your quest.

Listen to yourself when you describe what you are feeling.

If you are not fulfilled in your present work, then make a change.

Don't be afraid to leave home. Welcome the chance to do something totally new.

A call to serve is a call to prepare. That means study and practice.

Enjoy yourself. Serving God should make you feel satisfaction.

God has something special for you to do. Something about it will probably relate to missions. That is the most difficult calling because it requires crossing a culture, but it is the most thrilling.

At the age of ninety-five, Alma does not think much about the personal insults and set-backs she has suffered because of being a woman, an advocate for missions, an advocate for other women, an integrationist, and a defender of the downtrodden. Those pains, and the physical pains of old age, are conquered by the joy of welcoming each day as an opportunity to draw more of the world closer to the living God.

CHAPTER 9

# "God Does Indeed Call to Ministry Whom God Will, Gender Notwithstanding"

## MOLLY T. MARSHALL

Seeking God through serving the church has been my lifelong passion. One only seeks God because one is already sought, as the teachers of the faith have observed. My journey is a story of discerning that the regnant patriarchal structures of my ecclesial heritage were not God's ordained architecture, but a construction based on the fear of genuine equality between women and men. Because of a generous providence and a particular epoch in time, I have been graced to do what I believe God has called me to do—serve as a midwife of grace through theological education.

I grew up in northeastern Oklahoma, a place where Baptist piety allowed one a secure worldview. We knew what we were for, and more importantly, we knew what we were against. I can describe the place of my birth and growing up years in terms of two trails: the Trail of Tears and the Trail of Blood. The first trail refers to the deportation of the Cherokee Indians who were removed by government action in the 1830s from their homes in the Southeast and forced to travel by foot, wagon, and horseback halfway across the United States to a new land known as the Indian Territory. It was a cruel and harsh trek, and many died along the way; this tragic migration of Native Americans came to be known as the Trail of Tears. Many of the Cherokees settled in the area surrounding Muskogee, Oklahoma, my hometown. My great-grandfather, W. S. Wiley, was a missionary to the Indian Territory, sent by the Philadelphia Publication Society, to help start Sunday Schools and churches and to serve as a colporteur to distribute Christian literature among the Indians. I grew up with a sense of mission and the privilege of sharing the gospel with others. This is where the first trail converges with the second.

The kinds of Baptists that populated northeastern Oklahoma were of a conservative, if not fundamentalist, bent. Many of the Southern Baptists had imbibed a particular brand of Baptist heresy called Landmarkism. This view was popularized in the 1850s and spread south and westward from Kentucky and Tennessee. Landmark theology, or Baptist successionism as it was sometimes called, claimed that Baptists could be traced all the way back to the first century as the only true church.[1] Propagators of this form of Baptist triumphalism asserted that there was a "trail of blood" that ran through various sects and movements to Jesus' founding of the church. Thus there always had been a kind of "baptist" identity that kept the tradition of the early church unsullied—a claim that the Roman Catholics could not make. This trail was narrow, and church discipline kept the faithful on the way.

I grew up in a mission-minded, Bible-believing church that was loyal to the Southern Baptist Convention. It had a strong missionary organization for women and children. Of course, I completed all the "forward steps" of the Girls' Auxiliary, arriving at the esteemed level of "Queen Regent." Not surprising, the deacons were all men—as were the staff members, particularly those called "minister." Occasionally, there was a woman on the staff in other than a secretarial position; she was given the title "director" rather than minister, even though she might be functioning in a comparable way to a man who had held the same position before. Hence, male and female roles were clearly stratified, with men being seen as leaders and women as followers, except in the vital areas of missions and the educational ministries of the church. I never heard a woman pray in a worship service (except in a special prayer meeting or missionary testimony) until I was an adult. The uncertain message I received from that congregation was that there are things men can do, and women should not attempt to do them. I wondered about the justice of this, even as a youth. It seemed to me that if women had comparable seminary preparation and had sensed the calling of God, then churches would do well to receive them as the ministers God was providing.

As a twelve year old, I had a formative encounter with my pastor, Felix Wagner. It was youth week at church camp, and I was into my usual mischief. (I have been told that camp counselors drew lots to see which one got me for the week!) Brother Wagner (as we called him) stopped me on the way to the noon service for a brief chat. I wondered if I might be in some sort of trouble. Rather than correcting me for any disruption, he simply remarked, "You ought to think about working with young people when you grow up." It was a kind, indeed perceptive, word. He was suggesting that perhaps I had gifts to offer God in some kind of ministry. (I am sure that he had no inclination as to what lengths I might take that germinal idea!)

Two years later at age fourteen at another church camp, I distinctly felt the call of God to commit my life to "full-time Christian vocation." At that point all that I could imagine a woman being capable of or being permitted to do was missions or youth ministry. The encouraging words of my pastor came back to me as I made this commitment. My church was very affirming as I shared this decision upon my return from camp. One of the regular camp hymns was "Wherever He Leads I'll Go." It never occurred to me that I was disqualified from following simply because I was a girl or that I could not fully actualize this heartfelt decision.

My commitment did not waver, but I did receive some opposition from some of the "preacher boys" at Oklahoma Baptist

University, where I attended college. They were not convinced that God really called women to ministry, but if God did, it was with the understanding that women would serve under their ministerial authority (as wife or helper). I did not spend much time trying to refute their idea, although I was quite concerned about whether or not God's call to women was to be restricted in some manner. Further, the logic that these young men were using seemed to confuse women's role in the church and women's role in the home. They were trying to argue from the same notion of headship; that is, as the husband is head of the home, so the male pastor is head of the church. (Even then as a fledgling theologian, I perceived the logical fallacy—especially since the New Testament makes clear that Christ is the head of the church.) I also began to wonder what sort of "divine order" God really had in mind for the family. Their use of scripture was certainly self-serving in protecting male privilege, I concluded.

I spent each summer during college as a youth "director," leading Bible studies, planning and implementing youth activities, and helping adolescents learn about Christian service. My gifts for this kind of ministry were well received, unless I tried to speak in any official way from the pulpit. As long as I stuck to the area of youth programming I was fine; if I made any suggestion about the overall ministry of the congregation, I was seen as stepping out of my appropriate sphere of responsibility.

After college, I served at the First Baptist Church of Comanche, Texas, doing youth and community ministries. During that time, I began to sense that there was so much more to learn in order to be a reliable guide as a good minister of Christ Jesus. It was time to go to seminary, something I had been planning since I understood that God was beckoning me to ministry.

In 1973 I went to Southern Baptist Theological Seminary in Louisville, Kentucky, and became one of the first women to pursue a Master of Divinity degree. I went there because I knew I needed to grow in biblical and theological understanding; I also knew that I would be stretched beyond my provincial understanding. I had heard about a remarkable teacher there named Dale Moody, described by a former student as one who "loved the Bible and would make you think." I knew that I needed such a challenge to my faith.

It was not easy being one of only a handful of women in the M.Div. program. In some classes, I was the only woman, and some of my classmates were frankly puzzled, if not hostile, as to why I was pursuing the "pastor's" degree. Thankfully, at that time several of my professors, including Moody and Frank Stagg, were struggling with the role of women in ministry and beginning to write articles and monographs on the subject. As students we were blessed to hear them wrestle out loud in the classroom with the difficult texts and their own embedded theology. Both sides of the issue were regularly voiced in chapel sermons and student discussions. Because of the importance the biblical text holds in Baptist ecclesial tradition, I came to the point of saying that unless I believed scripture authorized the role of women in ministry, I could not in conscience pursue it further. Thankfully, Moody was of great assistance to me in this. One day he complimented me on a sermon I had preached in chapel, saying, "Molly, sometimes Christ is seen in the face of a woman." It was a word of graceful encouragement on my quest.

I was encouraged to pursue a Ph.D. at Southern, but in 1975 I did not have a sense of vocation as a theological educator, so I answered a call to be a minister of youth and single adults at the Pulaski Heights Baptist Church in Little Rock, Arkansas. There—in the context of an affirming church that permitted me to pray in morning worship, preach in evening worship, and be the spiritual guide for students, and in the context of a denomination that had begun to battle over the role of women in the church—I became absolutely persuaded through prayer, study, and personal experience that God does indeed call to ministry whom God will, gender notwithstanding.

And then the call of God came to me again. I believed that the Lord was beckoning me to return to school to prepare to be an equipper of ministers through theological education. I sensed that the role of women in the church would not perceptibly improve until seminaries moved into a more egalitarian structure with women joining men in the preparation of ministers. Although I considered other doctoral programs, I sensed that it might be wise to do my studies at the very place I desired, at some point, to join the faculty.

I returned to Southern Seminary to begin Ph.D. studies in theology in 1979. A few other women had already entered the doctoral program; however, there were no women yet teaching in the School of Theology, only in the Schools of Christian Education, Social Work, and Church Music. These courageous women had helped open the door for women to walk across another threshold.

As part of my doctoral study, I spent a semester at Cambridge University, where I met another teacher who made such an impact on my life. A renowned Anglican scholar, Bishop John A. T. Robinson was well ahead of most of his fellow clergymen in England in his clear advocacy for women in the priesthood. Although the ecclesial battle looked much different there, it was instructive to learn that throughout Christ's church the refreshing wind of the Spirit was stirring new life.

Robinson also taught me a great deal about contextual theology.[2] He understood that one's social location, gender, tradition, and ecclesial history contributed to a perspectival bias that one must not confuse with final truth. One's own religious experience cannot be claimed as normative for all others. Indeed, each of us has partial vision into the whole of God's truth, and we must seek it together. He also taught me to ask challenging questions that would help translate the melody of the gospel into a contemporary key. I am abidingly grateful for Robinson and Moody. I pray to bear the graceful marks of their influence in my own work as equipper of ministers.

About halfway through my doctoral dissertation, I began to apply for teaching positions. I received many rejections, usually on the premise that I lacked ministerial or teaching experience. To my chagrin, I discovered that some of these institutions hired males with much less experience than I for the jobs I had sought. It began to dawn on me that these institutions were afraid to hire a woman in a non-traditional field. I wondered if I had done all this graduate work for naught. I completed my doctoral exams and then my dissertation, but there was no academic position for me. All I knew to do was to follow the admonition I had learned in Sunday School: "Whatever thy hand findeth to do, do it with thy might." I learned of a small rural church, Jordan Baptist Church in Eagle Station, Kentucky, that needed an interim pastor, so I told them that "I would help them out until they could call a pastor."

At this point I was ordained by the St. Matthews Baptist Church in Louisville, Kentucky, a significant step I had considered for nearly a decade. I poured myself into sermon preparation, visitation, and community activities, and the little church began to grow stronger. To my surprise, about ten weeks after I started, the congregation decided to call me as its pastor. The rural parlance of the chair of the deacons, Eddie Lewis, articulated the church's decision, "If it ain't broke, don't fix it." I gladly accepted the call of that forward-thinking congregation. The members had discussed among themselves what it meant to exercise Baptist freedom; they could call whom they pleased to serve as their pastor. For the next year and a half, I labored as part-time pastor of Jordan Baptist Church. Some of the neighboring churches were a bit alarmed, but in the main they respected the local church autonomy that this church had exercised. By God's grace, I was ministering in the kind of setting to which my future students would be called; in God's wisdom, I was learning how to build the bridge from the classroom to the parish.

In 1984, about six months into this pastoral charge, Southern Seminary invited me to join the faculty as the first woman in the School of Theology. That I was ordained and was serving as a pastor *as a woman* became a point of great contention for fundamentalist critics of the seminary. Hostile letters to the president, provost, and dean—and to me—challenged the propriety of a woman teaching theology, "usurping authority over men." One distressed soul sent a letter to the dean inquiring, "Have you run out of intelligent men to teach our preacher boys?" Were I not such a sweet Christian, I would have responded to the letter with a couple of simple words—"Years ago."

Over the next eleven years, all my writings, addresses, and lectures were scrutinized by those looking for a way to condemn me. Although granted tenure in 1988 (which was a gigantic hurdle given the makeup of the board), I was well aware that no security existed for a seminary professor—especially one that wore skirts—in such an increasingly polarized convention. After President Roy Honeycutt retired, a young fundamentalist president, Albert Mohler, moved quickly to do the bidding of the board: "Get rid of that troublesome woman!" And he did within the first year of his presidency. So I left my spiritual home place where I had exercised my vocation as a midwife of grace. This departure has been well chronicled in other places, so I will not offer an *apologia* here.

The other theological institution in my story is Central Baptist Theological Seminary, where I have served as professor of theology and spiritual formation for nearly ten years. God preserved my vocation in theological education, for which I am deeply grateful. Thus, I can say with joy, "What others meant for me as evil, God meant for me as good." Just because one theological institution said a resounding "no" to my ministry of teaching did not mean that God did not want me to continue to serve in this way. God's providence opened another door for me to continue as a theological educator in the Baptist tradition.

Most recently I have been elected as the tenth president of this historic school. On January 1, 2005 I became the first woman to serve as president of a Baptist seminary in North America. The stained-glass ceiling has cracked a bit! This kind of gender sensitivity has long marked Central—there were women in the first class. Founded in 1901, Central served all the Baptists of this area for many years.[3] When Midwestern Baptist Theological Seminary was organized in the 1950s, the enrollment of Southern Baptist students dropped at Central. In more recent years, we have been a context where a "Baptist family reunion" has been taking place as Cooperative Baptists and American Baptists and National/Progressive Baptists take the voyage of theological education together.

Have there been challenges to following God's call? Of course there have! They have been wrenching and, at times, have eroded my self-esteem and caused great consternation. Most women are socialized to be agreeable, cooperative, and self-giving. We do not like to be the focus of controversy or suspicion; however, that is nearly inevitable at the beginning of any new movement. Briefly, I will note some of the challenges experienced by women in ministry.

The first is both a sociological and a theological challenge. For women to claim their rightful places in the church (or a theological institution) is to assume a certain teaching authority. Even at this late date in ecclesiastical history, many persons are not comfortable granting women authority in non-traditional fields. They somehow feel that men are more trustworthy, their voices more authoritative, and their judgment more rational and less emotional. Coupled with this is the regular and uncritical use of the old apostolic dictum: "I permit no woman to teach or have authority over a man."[4] Students at times resist taking instruction from a woman in theological studies, believing that women are not capable of the same scholarly rigor or theological insight as men. Perhaps they simply believe that learning from a woman is somehow demeaning and do not want to submit to her authority.

A second challenge is male ministerial colleagues who privately support a woman's calling, yet will not take a public stand for fear of ridicule from their male colleagues or of jeopardizing their own professional status. In earlier years I had colleagues distance themselves from me because they perceived I was a lightning rod and feared "guilt by association." Churches and institutions are always much more comfortable with "safe" ministers—those who avoid engaging thorny issues of justice and affirm the *status quo*. This is all the more so true when women enter the professional guild. Whereas churches or seminaries might tolerate men speaking prophetically about economic justice or equal rights, when women similarly address these issues, it is usually seen as strident, self-serving, or destabilizing behavior. When women believe that "keeping silent" no longer will do, they are usually considered a threat. This fear of women's strength continues to pervade most cultures.

A third challenge is closely related to the second. Women following their calling to ministry are often accused of pursuing a secular feminist agenda rather than faithfully responding to the beckoning of God. Thus, their motives are suspect, and the good they do is often discounted because of prejudice. I have been asked on more than one occasion: "Are you a feminist first or a Christian first?" The answer is straightforward: I am a feminist because I am a Christian. I became a feminist reading the apostle Paul, not Betty Friedan and Gloria Steinem.

A fourth challenge is more internal than external. Personal concerns that accompany women pursuing ministry have to do with issues of self-esteem, juggling home and family with church, lack of role models, and isolation. Because of the resistance many women have faced, they at times ask if there is something wrong with *them* rather than the patriarchal system that they are battling. One's sense of well-being can be compromised when this is protracted. Balancing the demands of home and family with work is the challenge of any professional man or woman; it is particularly daunting for the minister. The interruptive dimensions of a minister's work, including death and crisis, make this even more difficult for women because of the societal expectations about child-care and other responsibilities. Many women enter ministry without ever seeing another woman function as their present vocation dictates. Whereas men have received both formal and informal mentoring, women in ministry are still such a minority that most women have not had the degree of socialization toward the vocation needed. Finally, women who serve in a conference or association as the only woman pastor report a great sense of isolation.

So how can we address these challenges in a constructive way? This brief narrative closes with a few brief suggestions that can assist the new reformation stirred by the full inclusion of women as equal "partners in Christ's service," to use the words of Jane Parker Huber's hymn, "Called as Partners in Christ's Service."[5] As a theological educator, I believe that we are in a fruitful time for women in Baptist life.

First, let the seminary be a lab where men and women explore the theological and psychosocial dimensions of being colleagues in ministry. We must form new partnerships in ministry as women and men to demonstrate the great reconciliation of God. How we relate as faculty and students during these formative years will be crucial to ministry in the parish. Creative working relationships between male and female colleagues encourage learners to see a new horizon of promise.

Second, encourage a fresh consideration of the biblical materials. Wonderful new insights have emerged from feminist scholars and from recent attention to the social contexts of the Bible. Many persons who continue to resist the ministries of women do so because of faulty exegesis and an inadequate hermeneutical approach to scripture. God "hath more light to break forth from the Holy Scripture," as the English Separatist pastor John Robinson witnessed.

Third, women need to form groups to encourage and support their sisters' ministries. When you are a pioneer, it is very difficult to stay on course alone. Whether in church or seminary, groups that study, pray, and practice their new understanding together can do much to move the reformation forward. Our women in ministry group at Central Seminary continues to encourage faltering steps toward vocational fidelity.

Fourth, men need to learn to share their ecclesial authority gladly and generously. Whether in seminary or congregational context, men often have the power of place and can function as gatekeepers who can swing the door wide for women to enter. This kind of courageous stand will make a significant difference. Women cannot reform the church alone. Those who have more access to the corridors of power must open doors, serve as advocates, and offer encouragement to those newly given access to unfamiliar space. It is an important ministry for such a time as this.

Fifth and finally, we must depend upon God's help to bring about newness. God is doing a new thing in the church and is counting on us to participate in this reformation. May we have both wisdom and courage for the facing of this hour, for the renewal of the church, and for the sake of the Reign of God.

Not surprisingly, the narrative of my journey has ended with reflection on the role of theological education in creating a hospitable place for women to serve in all forms of ministry in Baptist life. For over twenty years I have witnessed the remarkable transformation that can occur in the lives of women as they learn new ways to read the texts used to bar them from pastoral work or as they discover their natural affinity for congregational leadership. I am grateful to be serving during this particular "hinge" time in Baptist life, a time when doors are opening to the fresh wind of God's Spirit evidenced in the lives of faithful sisters.

CHAPTER 10

# "I Wouldn't Take Nothing for My Journey": The Story of Ella Pearson Mitchell

## KEITH E. DURSO

Ella Pearson Mitchell has been called "a true matriarch of preaching"[1] and has been regarded as "the dean of black women preachers."[2] At the 1999 Hampton Ministers Conference, Hampton, Virginia, Ella was honored as "the mother of women preachers."[3] She is a woman who "belongs to that shining cadre of women who have courageously—and victoriously—confronted longstanding prejudices and sexist claims that the preaching function is the exclusive preserve of those who happen to born male."[4] Such praise seems natural for a woman who says that she "was literally born in the church."[5] Ella was born October 18, 1917, in the parsonage of Olivet Presbyterian Church, Charleston, South Carolina. Her father, Joseph R. Pearson, pastored that church for thirty-eight years. Ella began her ministry in her father's church when she was eight years old. She rode on the handlebars of her father's bicycle, accompanying him on pastoral visits to serve communion to shut-ins.[6]

As she grew older, Ella's Sundays became even busier. She provided music for services at her father's church and other churches in Charleston, sometimes attending six services on a Sunday.[7] She also spoke in the vesper meetings for youth. When she was older, her father's busy schedule proved beneficial to her. Pastor Pearson began serving a second church in Mt. Pleasant, South Carolina, and Ella often preached in his churches. She gained further ministerial experience while attending Talladega College in Talladega, Alabama, where she led the chapel services. Of that experience, Ella recalled, "I read the scripture, delivered messages, and sewed the cloth for the altar and the podium. You name it, I did it."[8]

At Talladega College Ella majored in religion and minored in science. Her majoring in religion was no small feat because the college did not offer a major in religion. However, she was determined to receive a degree in religion and waited patiently until the college hired professors to teach the necessary courses. During her senior year, the college finally hired two religion professors, and Ella crammed all of her religion courses into her senior year.[9]

After graduating from Talladega in 1939, Ella taught high school English for one year and then worked as a Sunday School missionary for another. During this time, she spoke at numerous conferences and meetings, and she felt the call to ministry. Although her father nurtured and encouraged her calling, Ella's mother did not. Ella said that her mother "was dying inside, and when I went to seminary she just about flipped."[10] Ella explained to her mother that Jesus was a teacher and that was what she wanted to be. Such an explanation, however, did not calm Mrs. Pearson's anxiety.

In 1941 Ella applied to Yale University Divinity School. Citing few field work opportunities for African American men in the New Haven area, and even fewer for African American women, leaders at the divinity school suggested that she apply to Union Theological Seminary in New York, which she did.[11] Ella matriculated as a religious education major in 1941. Despite expressing her call to teach, she soon discovered that even the teaching ministry was not open to women. "At Union," she said, "the dean told us we were there to find husbands, and I was steered toward Christian education. I never considered the pastorate because no one steered me in that direction. All women did Christian education then."[12]

During her years at Union, Ella served as the assistant to the pastor at St. James Presbyterian Church in New York City. She led the morning worship services and often preached at the evening services.[13] In 1943 Ella graduated with an M.A. from Union, making her one of the first African Americans to graduate from that seminary. She then served for two years as minister of education at the Church of the Master (Presbyterian) in New York City. Her primary responsibility was "girls work."[14] The church licensed her to preach in 1943. Ella then asked to be ordained to the teaching ministry. The Presbyterian leaders, however, put off granting her request and never ordained her.[15]

The following year, Ella married Henry Mitchell, whom she had met at Union. Along with her change in marital status came a change in her denominational status. Because Henry was a Baptist, Ella became a Baptist, and Henry had the privilege of baptizing her by immersion.[16] At each of her husband's pastorates, she served mainly in the areas of Christian education and music.[17] Together they have ministered in churches and in several educational institutions over the past sixty years. Ella and Henry have often preached dialogue sermons, or what they call "team preaching," in which they alternate speaking and at times speak in unison.[18] Samuel K. Roberts, a friend and colleague of the Mitchells, described both of them as "preachers of great power and passion."[19]

In the 1970s, because of the influence of the women's liberation movement, Ella's activity in the National Council of Churches, and her service on the board of publication in the American Baptist Churches, Ella preached and taught often. After several years of such service, she began to explore the possibility of ordination. She noted, "I felt I wanted to be ordained. What a struggle."[20]

After her mother died in mid-1970s, Ella felt free to pursue ordination in a Baptist church. In her sermon "Whom God Chooses, God Uses," in which she referred to herself as "that woman," Ella described her call to preach and to ordination:

> That woman continued to resist a call to preach even after seminary preparation, teaching in seminaries, and through the years of delivering the "Word." Then one Sunday morning [in 1973] fifty years after her first word from the Lord, the Holy Ghost just snatched her out of the pew. She went running down the aisle to tearfully confess her "call to preach." God insisted and the Holy Spirit moved to the ordination. God be praised! God has chosen her, and God does move in mysterious yet powerful ways.[21]

One Baptist minister agreed to ordain her. Later, however, he backed out because, he said, the Holy Spirit had told him not to do it. The same day he refused to ordain her, another minister, J. Alfred Smith Sr., told Ella that he would ordain her. In October 1978, after thirty-five years of ministry, Ella was ordained at Allen Temple Baptist Church in Oakland, California.[22]

The hesitancy of the Presbyterians and the refusal of the Baptist pastor to ordain Ella illustrate the opposition to women ministers that she encountered throughout her many years of ministry. She believed that such opposition, "as…Blacks know so well," has been "a game of power."[23] While acknowledging the contributions of African American churches in civil rights and socio-political matters, Ella maintained that these churches "lag far behind in applying" justice and equality "to women. This applies most specifically to the professional options open to women. For instance, there are still rigid exclusions of women from ordination and from placement in pulpits and pastorates of African American churches. In this area, equality is still the exception and not the rule."[24] She further noted, "Our professional careers have seemed stymied repeatedly by racism, sexism, and just plain Black-on-Black pettiness."[25]

Unlike some denominations that have bishops who can move churches along faster, Baptists, and particularly Black Baptists, according to Ella, are slower to accept women ministers partly because many pastors suffer from severe cases of job insecurity. Without a bishop and a guaranteed appointment, and many without professional ministerial training, many African American pastors "serve at all times in fear of sudden and permanent unemployment. The highly impressive gifts of so many second-career African American women often terrify these insecure men. Since they dare not be candid, the easiest defense is a rigid, surface biblical justification for the exclusion of women from the pulpit."[26]

Ella has experienced such pastoral pettiness and insecurity throughout her ministry. Many churches welcomed her into their services, not to preach, but to give a "message." While teaching religious education at the Berkley Baptist Divinity School (now the American Baptist Seminary of the West), she "preached all over" California, "most of the time on women's day. I did not call it preaching, I would give…the women's day message, youth day message or some other message. It was never a sermon."[27] In some churches, as long as she spoke from somewhere other than behind the pulpit, she was welcome. On more than one occasion, she was asked "to preach from the floor."[28] Yet such opposition did not stop Ella from preaching or the Spirit from working. She remembered:

> One Sunday when a licensed preacher presiding from the lofty pulpit ordered me to speak from the floor of the sanctuary and decreed that he would extend the invitation. When I had finished speaking from the text "We have these treasures in earthen vessels" [2 Cor 4:7], he sensed that it would be utter nonsense for him to intervene. He signaled for me to open the doors of the church, which I did. The response to that invitation still brings a warm affirmation to my ministry, for *four* adult men and one young woman came forward—three of the men and the woman as candidates for baptism and the fourth man coming by Christian experience.[29]

Opposition to women preachers, however, is not confined to men. Women, too, fear them. Ella lamented, "Although we women are in the numerical and financial majority in our churches, a great many of us, like some of the slaves, love our chains and shackles too well to change."[30]

With so many barriers preventing women access to ministerial positions, what will help African American women gain entry into those positions in Black Baptist churches? Ella's greatest challenge as a woman in ministry "has been trying to find ways to help women who believe that they have felt the call. Many have not had any support. I search for ways to convince them to go on. I search for...the right words to say." One of those words is patience. She has advised women "to wait on the Lord and don't push the situation. If they push the situation, they will usually end up set back, slowed down, and set aside because they couldn't wait until God opened a door or a window."[31] Many feminists who advocate a more aggressive approach will not accept such counsel. While aware that women comprise an "oppressed body," Ella has insisted that women must "believe that God has prophesied our liberation; God has declared what he *will* do *in* us and *with* us, and we know that liberation will come to pass. It may be evidenced by a number of means, in a number of ways, but it will come. I would hate to see it come to pass by a mass revolution, and I don't suspect it ever will."[32] "A tone of hostile militance," she warned, "will hardly serve the purpose of God or of women, and black women should be more aware of this than most. Muscle alone cannot bring about just access to the role of preacher. But by the grace of God, love and superior performance may achieve our goal."[33]

Another word of advice Ella has given to women is to prepare for ministry, and to prepare means that women must acquire the necessary theological training.[34] Such training will hone the gifts God has given them and will help them achieve excellence in their ministries. "Excellence," she said, "transcends its detractors, and in the end it will conquer, moving past opposition to be used by God." Unlike men, women "cannot afford the luxury of mediocrity."[35]

Although placing a higher standard for women to achieve is unjust, Ella has noted that such a standard is not another roadblock but an opportunity for God to do a great work: "God did not wish that we women be so burdened, but God reserves the right to wring from this cross a blessing for us as well as for the church. In a day when the church is more threatened than ever, it may be that it requires more dedication and preparation than ever.... We women are challenged to exceed the minimum and break down the walls of gender discrimination through excellence of preparation and practice in ministry."[36]

Even though everyone will not change their minds concerning women ministers, some will. Ella recalled an incident from one of her preaching-from-the-floor experiences that changed one male preacher's mind. This pastor told her that if she preached in his church, she would have to do it from the floor. So from the floor she preached. After the sermon, the pastor told her, "'I changed my mind. Anyone who can preach like that should be doing it from the pulpit.'"[37]

A third word of advice is providence—trust in God's leadership. Despite the many barriers opponents to women ministers have constructed through the centuries, Ella has reminded women that "the enemies have not been able to close all the doors" because "when they slam one, God seems to open another."[38] According to Ella, God has always willed that women be ministers, and although the Bible is not as clear on this subject as she might like it to be, she looked to Peter's sermon on Pentecost, in which he proclaimed that God promised to pour out the Holy Spirit on "all flesh," which encompasses both men and women.[39] In God's pouring, Ella contended, God "has dumped the bucket on a whole lot of women a whole lot of times.... This is in the mind and will of God, and God who changeth not has never willed it otherwise. It's we faltering humans who have the hangups."[40]

Yet even in cultures where the subordination of women has been etched in stone, if we look hard enough, Ella insisted, we can see "blinding shafts of light indicating that God is breaking through those cultural biases and progressively revealing himself in ever higher dimensions in regard to women—just as God has done in regard to minorities."[41] Deborah, Huldah, Pricilla, the Corinthian women prophets, and Philip's daughters are just a few of such "blinding shafts of light" in the Bible.[42] God's inclusion of these women demonstrates that God is indiscriminate, for God is no respecter of persons. Any discrimination we encounter is human created, not God ordained.[43] Ella pointed to her own life to demonstrate how God uses persons whom society and even the church deem unusable. "What committee," she asked, "would have selected a chubby girl converted in Charleston, South Carolina, in 1925 to be a kind of entering wedge for the breaking of the barrier against women?"[44]

Ella noted that she firmly believes that God will fulfill his word spoken through the prophet Joel,[45] for "God has never been a respecter of persons. We are God's children created in his image, and God's will has not changed. This is not just wishful thinking. This is the prophetic *word* of God. This will be! Prophecy has always been for right and righteousness. Prophecy has always suggested the ultimate triumph of God."[46] For that Ella has been grateful; after all, "God is not about to waste half of God's gifts and talents because they are not used in the male-dominated tradition."[47]

In offering sound guidance to women entering the ministry, Ella encouraged them with these words: Be certain of your calling, ignore your detractors, and find support groups. Women must be certain that they "have gotten the appointment from God to run this marathon" and that they "are representing God."[48] Such advice will help women when they encounter persons who say that women cannot or should not preach. Yet "what makes them think that they can decide who should preach?" Ella asked incredulously. Also, instead of worrying about what detractors think, she encouraged women to "lift up the Bible for men and women and show them the biblical examples of women who have carried the Good News, the gospel."[49] Do not let them steal your joy of preaching.[50] Finally, Ella acknowledged that she is fortunate to have had a husband and a father who supported her, and she suggested that women surround themselves with encouragers to strengthen them on their journey.[51] She has encouraged women, "Join a support group. Lean on friends, supportive spouses, and some pastors."[52]

Despite the many barriers women in ministry face, Ella remained optimistic for the future of women ministers. "The future is bright" in the African American church, she said, because many of those barriers have been broken down and more women are serving as pastors and can serve as role models for other women. Many denominations "are on the move," and the future in them for women is bright. "Baptists," however, "still lag far behind."[53]

Ella's optimism is based on four factors that will continue to create more ministerial opportunities for Baptist women. First, the network of supportive male and female pastors is growing. Second, women can take advantage of the ministry opportunities currently open to them so that churches will be exposed to their gifts and talents. Third, some opposing pastors will change their minds. When a daughter or a strong church member "hears the call," such pastors will be forced to rethink their position on women in ministry. Finally, as the number of women theological students increase, future male pastors will experience personally the giftedness and the calling of their female colleagues. "With all of these factors," Ella said, "the future is not as dark as it might have been, and the huge reservoir of God-given gifts among female potential leaders may yet be utilized to save and enrich the African American churches."[54]

Churches, however, might still be hesitant to call a woman minister. To such churches Ella offered this advice: Focus on the positives women bring to the pulpit, not on their perceived "baggage." She noted that women "bring to the pulpit their intuition, their passion, and the ability to express the love of God in a way that men can't. The mother in me believes that. I'd tell the church to not worry about what it thinks women bring to the pulpit as baggage. Women are mothers, and as mothers role models. They need to be seen as mothers of the gospel and gospel-proclaiming role models."[55]

To men and women who continue to focus on past injustices, Ella also offered a word to them. They should "focus on the future. The goal is the prize of the high calling. Philippians 4 is a chapter I love to preach from. It calls us to service, tells us not to dwell on the past, and tells us to press, press, for the mark of the high calling. We would do well to do that."[56] However, to men and women who despair for the future, Ella would say to them that "when God calls and faith responds, human forecasts are transcended." The current circumstances are much more favorable than when, on faith, she started ministering as an eight-year-old child in 1925.[57]

The story of Ella Pearson Mitchell has been a blessing to untold numbers of people. For more than sixty years she has labored tirelessly to open the doors of opportunity for the women who have followed her.[58] As Patricia A. Gould-Champ observed, Ella "is the epitome of the preacher who receives the Word and brings that word forth in the totality of who she is as a woman. Ella Mitchell reminds us of the wonderful thing God has done in calling women to preach. She challenges preachers, women and men alike, to offer no less than our best. For this we are eternally thankful. She is the best of *Those Preachin' Women!*"[59]

Yet Ella's story has also been a blessed one, as she has readily admitted. Reflecting on her long ministry, a ministry in which she has served as a preacher, a teacher, and an educator, she said, "Through the years I have grown from a Southern underprivileged Black girl to maturity as a serving Christian woman.... I feel fulfilled. 'I wouldn't take nothing for my journey.' It has been blessed."[60]

CHAPTER 11

# "I Am Female, But God Knew That Before He Called Me": The Story of Ruby Welsh Wilkins

JOHN PIERCE

When Ruby Welsh Wilkins married in 1940, she joined the Beulah Congregational Church near Wadley, Alabama, where her husband's family had roots. But she could never get over the fact that she was a Baptist. "It seems like once you're a Baptist, you're always a Baptist," said Wilkins, a soft-spoken octogenarian, reflecting upon her incredible faith journey. "Baptists seem to be truer in doctrine than other denominations."[1]

Ruby felt the urge to visit the struggling Antioch Baptist Church down Highway 22. She never dreamed that the church would become such a vital part of her life—and the idea that she would serve as pastor of that rural congregation for more than thirteen years was beyond the realm of possibilities. "The church [organized in 1897] was on the verge of collapsing in the '40s," Ruby recalled. Only the faithfulness of a widow named Mrs. Sanders and her daughter, Vashti, kept the doors open.

Ruby and her sister-in-law, who was also raised Baptist, began to help. "Sunday after Sunday, we would come up here and have Sunday School," she remembered. A Vacation Bible School was also held in the summer of 1950, but Ruby was unable to help. She had just given birth to her third son. The church "began to get a little life breathed into it," Ruby recalled, but then the church building burned down. The cause of the fire was never determined, but the determination of this small band of Baptists increased. "That church burning started building a fire under us," said Ruby, who helped collect donations to rebuild. The white frame church building was completed in 1951, and the congregation began to grow. "Mrs. Sanders saw to it that we cooperated with the [Tallapoosa Baptist] Association," Ruby remembered. "We got the church coming along and had several different pastors—all were good men."

An unexpected experience a couple of years earlier had reinforced Ruby's spiritual commitment. But she was unsure how her affirmation of a call to ministry would work out. "It was in 1948 that the Lord called me," said Ruby. "I had been going through a turbulent time in my own life,...[but] I kept hearing the Lord say there was something for me to do. I cried out 'Lord, what is it that you want me to do?' and he said, 'Feed my sheep.' But I was a woman. I was amazed. It was part disbelief. I couldn't understand because of my Baptist upbringing."

"I was saved in a Baptist church in Daviston, [Alabama]," Ruby recalled, but members of that church "had always assumed God didn't call women to the pulpit. God called women to missions. It seemed so out of line, but I couldn't dispute it. I'd heard that voice before. It was not an audible voice. But the night I was saved, I was nine years old, and I heard 'What do you want to do with Jesus?' There was an urgency in that voice. I responded, 'I want Jesus.' And he's been with me ever since."

Ruby said that she struggled with how to fulfill her calling and with whom to share it. In addition to her husband, Millard, who "had no objections," she told her parents of her calling. "I didn't know how they would be, but they were very sympathetic." Her father, a Baptist deacon and writer of gospel songs, "didn't doubt that I was called," she added. Still uncertain about how her calling would take shape, Ruby poured herself into the study of scripture and teaching the mixed-gender adult Sunday School class at Antioch. It was a position she held for twelve years.

"I had taught this class knowing all the time that God had called me," said Ruby. "I thought maybe this was what God wanted, but I began to sense there was something else." Sometimes the pastor would attend the class, she recalled. Once he commented, "Miss Ruby can make a sermon out of any Sunday School text. But we Baptists don't have women preachers." "He was one of my favorite preachers," she remembered with a smile. Feeling a strong calling to preach, yet realistic enough to believe what her pastor had said, Ruby and her husband began attending a church of a different denomination known for its openness to women ministers. "I wasn't happy there," she recalled. "I never felt welcome among their male clergy."

Though committed to her bedrock Baptist beliefs, Ruby said that she always enjoyed worship and fellowship with other Christians. "Mrs. Sanders was so denominational oriented, but I'm not," she said. "I can have fellowship with other churches." But Ruby's firm convictions kept drawing her back into the Baptist fold even though her ministerial calling was often rebuffed.

One of those convictions was the doctrine of eternal security she had embraced from her Baptist upbringing. "I can't find in my Bible where there's teaching for anything else," said Ruby. "Once you're saved, the Holy Spirit kicks in and does his work.... We are not kept by any works we do." Not all policies and practices at her little Baptist church made sense to Ruby, however. Such was the case when her husband joined Antioch and was re-baptized in a nearby creek although he had been immersed as a believer in another denomination. "I think one immersion is necessary," said Ruby. "If Jesus wasn't immersed, why did he go *into* the River Jordan. They could have taken a pitcher upon the bank. But if you're saved before you're baptized, then that one immersion should suffice. That's one thing I had against the Baptists. Mrs. Sanders and others [at Antioch] were strict about that."

They were also strict about "closed communion," only welcoming Baptists to participate in the Lord's Supper, and Ruby disagreed with that practice as well. "It's the Lord's table, not the Baptists'," said Ruby matter-of-factly. "I really had more against the Baptists, but the one thing I had for them was important."

In the late 1960s Antioch Baptist Church appeared to have run its course as a "springboard for young preachers in the association." There was talk of closing the doors. In 1970 Ruby started running a little publication titled *The Commission Church Woman* off an old mimeograph machine. "I'd put a little sermon in each one," she said. "Before I could get out the November [1970] issue, this little group [from Antioch] asked me to come [back]."

Ruby resumed teaching the adult Bible class though the church had no pastor or worship services. The remnant dreamed of reestablishing the church, but "decided they didn't want another man to come up here from the association." After Ruby taught the lessons each Sunday morning for another year, some began to ask: "Why not organize and become a church again?" "So we did," said Ruby. "We got our slate of officers elected, and I was the pastor. I knew I was called."

The church contacted the associational missionary, Donald Bailey, to see if he could help with Ruby's ordination. Bailey was supportive, she said. "He talked to pastors and couldn't get them to agree to it [though] it would have been all right with him." The church had given Ruby her ministerial license when it reorganized, but the members wanted wider participation in her ordination. Their efforts to involve churches of the association, however, faced "stumbling blocks."

Ruby contacted the late Baptist scholar Frank Stagg and his wife, Evelyn, knowing of their support of women ministers. The Staggs were so impressed by Ruby's calling and commitment that they paid her a visit. "Dr. Stagg didn't think ordination was all that important,"

Ruby recalled. "He didn't put all that much emphasis on ordination, but women in ministry do." So Ruby and her church decided to focus on the ministry at hand and not be concerned with her lack of ordination, and under her leadership the church prospered. The church building was refurbished, and Ruby stayed busy. She preached a revival, baptized new converts, and performed funerals.

Affirmation of her ministry from fellow Southern Baptists was rare. But to Ruby, the criticism she received just did not make good sense. For years she had been warmly affirmed for her insightful Bible teaching and for the inspirational poems she penned and sent to friends each Christmas and some Easters. "My poetry can be accepted, but my preaching can't," said Ruby. "But it all comes from the same source." And the resistance was not only from men. "Baptist women in a sense are as bad or maybe worse in being against women pastors," she said. "At least that's been my experience." However, Ruby was not deterred from her calling. "It was a long time [between calling and the pastorate], but I've raised four boys—I was a busy mother." She also worked full time at a sewing plant, in addition to her responsibilities at home and church.

Ruby's service as pastor of Antioch Baptist Church near Wadley, Alabama, lasted more than thirteen years (from 1971–1984) until her husband's Alzheimer's disease became so severe that he needed full-time care. "There wasn't any way I could keep the church going and care for him," she recalled. She buried her husband in the small church cemetery in 1985.

After her husband's death, Ruby decided to fulfill one of her lifelong dreams. She enrolled in college. When she graduated from Daviston high school in the late 1930s, her parents could not afford to send her to college, so at the age of seventy-two, Ruby for the first time registered as a college student at Southern Union State Junior College in Wadley. She soon completed her associate's degree and graduated with a 4.0 grade point average.

Though now a widow and a retired pastor, Ruby occasionally gets a call to help with a funeral or shed a little light on a biblical text.

"I don't profess to know much about the Bible, but I have that name around here," she admitted. "A lot of people call me about things they don't understand. It all goes back to the Lord. I'd never been a consistent Bible student until I was called." However, her deep love for the Bible goes back to childhood. Ruby once asked her mother if she could have a Bible if she read it through. "She said 'Yes,' and I still have it. At first, I kept reading the book of Genesis and then stopping," Ruby recalled with a smile. "But I've since learned that reading the book of Genesis is where the foundation is laid."

Critics who claim that women ministers are driven by personal ambition would have an impossible case with Ruby. She never aspired to the pulpit or mapped a course of action to get there. "I didn't have any teacher but the Holy Spirit," said Ruby. "I didn't go buy a lot of books someone else had written. I just used the Word and the Holy Spirit, and that's where I learned what little I know."

Public speaking did not come easy either. When standing to give an address as valedictorian of her high school class, Ruby forgot what she had planned to say. "I wondered how I was ever going to give a sermon," she recalled. "But I'd forgotten that I'm not the one doing it. I knew that [God] was able, but I had not yet proved him."

After her retirement, Ruby said a fundamentalist preacher assumed the Antioch pastorate. He would leave the large pulpit Bible open to Paul's assertion that women should be silent in church, she recalled with a chuckle. "I'm a firm believer in laughter," she added. "The qualifications for preachers and deacons outlined by Paul—well, I've never seen anybody who lives up to those." Her successor's efforts lasted only a few months, said Ruby, before the church was in decline once again.

Through the years, other families in the community have called on her in times of need. But the church once again faced the likely possibility of closing its doors forever. In 2004 the church building was in need of repair, but Ruby continued to keep the lights on and the doors open by personally paying the electricity and insurance bills. She remembered how a dedicated widow and her daughter kept the church going through lean times. Without their commitment, Ruby knew that she would not have had many years of meaningful ministry at Antioch. So she and her youngest son, Mark, faithfully make their way to the old church building every Sunday morning. "Mark reads the Sunday School lesson from *Baptists Today*, and we discuss it," said Ruby. And occasionally others come by to join them.

Despite the small numbers at the church, Ruby, now eighty-six years old, continues to be optimistic. One Sunday, nine persons were present, including two young brothers who were sensing a call to ministry. Ruby suggested that Antioch might be a good place for them to get some experience preaching and, in turn, an opportunity for the church to come to life once again. Perhaps they realized as well that this quiet country church could be an even better place to find a mentor in ministry who knows the virtue of being faithful to a divine calling.

"It's strange how God times things," Ruby said. Her calling preceded her pastoral ministry by twenty-two years, and she now urges other women ministers to persevere as she did. "If you're called, you know," Ruby said. "But not everybody around you agrees." Ruby did not set out to be a trailblazer for female Baptist ministers. She just wanted to be faithful to what she considers a clear calling to "feed the sheep." "I am female, but God knew that before he called me," said Ruby. "So evidently, that was no determining factor to him." She has described her call as "too clear, too definite and too urgent" to be mistaken.

Ruby believes that Baptist churches are becoming more open to women in the pulpit and celebrates every hopeful sign. "I was so elated," she said, when learning that the Baptist Church of the Covenant in downtown Birmingham had called Sarah Jackson Shelton as pastor in 2002. "I was just overjoyed." Ruby acknowledged that churches are slow to change, but she is convinced that change is slowly coming. "It takes the truth a long time to catch up," she said. "Baptists one day are going to wake up and realize that women preachers are not in the same group as liberalists." Resistance from other Christians should not deter one's response to a divine calling, she added. "I can take whatever people dish out. Look at what they did to Jesus. If I can suffer along with him, I consider it a privilege. I've had to do what he wanted me to do. That is my main concern." Ruby even expects leaders of the Southern Baptist Convention—who made opposition to women pastors an official doctrinal position in 2000—to have a change of heart. "I believe that someday Southern Baptists will accept women fully in the ministry," she said. "It won't be in my lifetime." Does she expect them to formally apologize to women in the same way they recanted of racism in 1995? "I don't care if they apologize—acceptance will be enough for me."

# Baptist Women in the United States

## A Selected Bibliography from 1970 to 2005

Adams, Sheri. *What the Bible Really Says about Women*. Macon GA: Smyth & Helwys, 1994.

Allen, Catherine B. *A Century to Celebrate: History of Woman's Missionary Union*. Birmingham AL: Woman's Missionary Union, 1987.

———. "Diverse Baptist Attitudes toward Women in Missions." *Baptist History and Heritage* 38/3 (Summer/Fall 2002): 76–88.

———. "A Historical Survey of Women in Southern Baptist Life." In *The Role of Women in Southern Baptist Life*, 4–10. Nashville: Sunday School Board of the Southern Baptist Convention, 1988.

———. "The Impact of Southern Baptist Women on Social Issues: Other Issues Needing Attention." *Baptist History and Heritage* 22/3 (July 1987): 36–40.

———. *Laborers Together with God: 22 Great Women in Baptist Life*. Birmingham AL: Woman's Missionary Union, 1987.

———. "The Role of Women in Nonvocational Leadership." In *The Role of Women in Southern Baptist Life*, 12–18. Nashville: Sunday School Board of the Southern Baptist Convention, 1988.

———. "The Role of Women in the Support of Missions." In *The Role of Women in Southern Baptist Life*, 19–25. Nashville: Sunday School Board of the Southern Baptist Convention, 1988.

———. "The Role of Women in Vocational Missions." In *The Role of Women in Southern Baptist Life*, 26–30. Nashville: Sunday School Board of the Southern Baptist Convention, 1988.

———. "What Southern Baptist Women Need to Know about Denominational Structure (Politics)." *Called and Committed*. May 1979. 1–2.

———. "Women in Church-Related Vocations, Consultation On." In *Encyclopedia of Southern Baptists*, 4:2558–59. Nashville: Broadman Press, 1982.

———. "Women's Movements and Southern Baptists." In *Encyclopedia of Southern Baptists*, 4:2560–62. Nashville: Broadman Press, 1982.

"American Baptist Churches Task Force on Women." *American Baptist Quarterly* 20/3 (September 2001): 252–55.

Anders, Sarah Frances. "Woman's Role in the Southern Baptist Convention and Its Churches as Compared with Selected Other Denominations." *Review and Expositor* 72/1 (Winter 1975): 31–39.

———. "Women in Ministry: The Distaff Side of the Church." *Review and Expositor* 80/3 (Summer 1983): 427–36.

Anderson, Barbara. "From World Wide Guild to AB GIRLS: ABW's Ministry to Girls through the Years." *American Baptist Quarterly* 20/3 (September 2001): 298–315.

Anderson, Fred. "In Our Mother's Gardens." *Review and Expositor* 95/3 (Summer 1998): 349–63.

Beck, Rosalie. "The Impact of Southern Baptist Women on Social Issues: Human Rights." *Baptist History and Heritage* 22/3 (July 1987): 29–32.

———. "A Response to 'The Ordination of Women Among Texas Baptists' by Ann Miller." *Perspectives in Religious Studies* 29/3 (Fall 2002): 289–93.

———. "Signs of Peace and Sanity: Baptist Women and World War II." *Baptist History and Heritage* 36/3 (Summer/Fall 2001): 44–56.

———. "Texas Baptist Women between the Wars: Invisible Women." *Texas Baptist History* 8 (1988): 10–17.

———. "Women in the Life and Work of the Southern Baptist Convention." In *The Role of Women in Southern Baptist Life*, 39–45. Nashville: Sunday School Board of the Southern Baptist Convention, 1988.

Bellinger, Libby. "More Hidden than Revealed: The History of Southern Baptist Women in Ministry." In *The Struggle for the Soul of the SBC: Moderate Responses to the Fundamentalist Movement*, edited by Walter B. Shurden, 129–50. Macon GA: Mercer University Press, 1993.

Bentall, Shirley F. "Baptists and 'Freedom of Expression without Distinction as to…Sex.'" In *Faith, Life, and Witness: The Papers of the Study and Research Division of the Baptist World Alliance, 1986–1990*, edited by William H. Brackney, 275–86. Birmingham AL: Samford University Press, 1990.

Bentley, Eljee. "Women of the Southern Baptist Convention." In *Faith, Life, and Witness: The Papers of the Study and Research Division of the Baptist*

*World Alliance, 1986–1990*, edited by William H. Brackney, 138–46. Birmingham AL: Samford University Press, 1990.

Blevins, Carolyn DeArmond. "Diverse Baptist Attitudes toward Women in Ministry." *Baptist History and Heritage* 38/3 (Summer/Fall 2002): 71–76.

———. "Ordination of Women: Wrong or Right?" *The Theological Educator* 37 (Spring 1988): 100–11.

———. "Patterns of Work Among Southern Baptist Women." *Baptist History and Heritage* 22/3 (July 1987): 41–49.

———. "Reflection: Baptists and Women's Issues in the Twentieth Century." *Baptist History and Heritage* 35/3 (Summer/Fall 2000): 53–66.

———. "The Role of Women in Religious Education." In *The Role of Women in Southern Baptist Life*, 32–38. Nashville: Sunday School Board of the Southern Baptist Convention, 1988.

———. "Women and the Baptist Experience." In *Religious Institutions and Women's Leadership: New Roles Inside the Mainstream*, edited by Catherine Wessinger, 158–80. Columbia: University of South Carolina Press, 1996.

———. "Women in Baptist History." *Review and Expositor* 83/1 (Winter 1986): 51–61.

———. *Women in Christian History: A Bibliography*. Macon GA: Mercer University Press, 1995.

———. *Women's Place in Baptist Life*. The Baptist Heritage Library. Brentwood TN: Baptist History and Heritage, 2003.

Bradley, Martia. "The Work and Witness of Southern Negro Baptist Women from 1865 Until 1935." *The Quarterly Review* 37/1 (October–December 1976): 53–60.

Bridges, Linda McKinnish. "Women in Church Leadership." *Review and Expositor* 95/3 (Summer 1998): 327–47.

Chandler, Charles H. "What about Women Deacons?" *Search* 8/3 (Spring 1979): 24–41.

———. "What about Women Deacons?" *The Deacon* 14/3 (April–June 1984): 45–50.

Clanton, Jana Aldredge. "Why I Believe Southern Baptists Churches Should Ordain Women." *Baptist History and Heritage* 23/3 (July 1988): 52–54.

Cook, L. Katherine. "Texas Baptist Women and Missions, 1830–1900." *Texas Baptist History* 3 (1983): 31–46.

Crumpler, Carolyn Weatherford. "The Role of Women in Baptist
    Missions." *Baptist History and Heritage* 27/3 (July 1992): 25–33.

Davis, C. Anne. "Women, Ordination of Southern Baptist." In *Encyclopedia
    of Southern Baptists*, 4:2557–58. Nashville: Broadman Press, 1982.

Deichmann, Wendy J. "Domesticity with a Difference: Woman's Sphere,
    Women's Leadership, and the Founding of the Baptist Missionary
    Training School." *American Baptist Quarterly* 9/3 (September 1990):
    141–57.

Deweese, Charles W. "Deaconesses in Baptist History: A Preliminary
    Study." *Baptist History and Heritage* 12/1 (January 1977): 52–57.

———. *Women Deacons and Deaconesses: 400 Years of Baptist Service*. Macon
    GA: Mercer University Press, 2005.

Durso, Pamela R. "Diverse Baptist Attitudes toward Women in Theological
    Education." *Baptist History and Heritage* 38/3 (Summer/Fall 2002):
    62–71.

Falls, Helen Emery. "Baptist Women in Missions Support in the
    Nineteenth Century." *Baptist History and Heritage* 12/1 (January 1977):
    26–36.

Filipi, Emily. "What's Happening to the Women?" *The Quarterly Review*
    30/2 (April–June 1970): 35–37.

Flemister, L. Faye. "The Impact of a Conscience." *American Baptist
    Quarterly* 20/3 (September 2001): 256–66.

Gaskin, J. M. *Baptist Women in Oklahoma*. Oklahoma City: Messenger Press,
    1985.

Gray, James R. "Ordination: Male or Female." *The Southern Baptist Journal*
    5/2 (March 1977): 9.

Harris, Anne Cheves. "Working Hand to Hand: An Overview of the
    Ecumenical Witness of American Baptist Women." *American Baptist
    Quarterly* 20/3 (September 2001): 270–78.

Higginbotham, Evelyn Brooks. *Righteous Discontent: The Women's Movement
    in the Black Baptist Church, 1880–1920*. Cambridge MA: Harvard
    University Press, 1993.

Hoadley, Frank T., and Benjamin P. Browne. *Baptists Who Dared*. Valley
    Forge PA: Judson Press, 1980.

Holcomb, Carol Crawford. "'Coming into a New Awareness': Women
    Deacons at Seventh and James Baptist Church." *Texas Baptist History* 18
    (1998): 1–25.

———. "The Kingdom at Hand: The Social Gospel and the Personal Service Department of Woman's Missionary Union, Auxiliary to the Southern Baptist Convention." *Baptist History and Heritage* 35/2 (Spring 2000): 49–66.

Holt, Sally Dean Smith. "The SBC and the WMU: Issues of Power and Authority Relating to Organization and Structure." Ph.D. dissertation, Vanderbilt University, 2001.

Hull, William E. "Women and the Southern Baptist Convention." *Christian Ethics Today* 6/4 (August 2004): 10–17.

Jennings, Susan Lea. "Honourable Women: The Varied Roles of Women within the Southern Baptist Convention." Master's thesis, Appalachian State University, 1998.

Kaemmerling, Charlene. "Ordination of Women: Wrong or Right?" *The Theological Educator* 37 (Spring 1988): 93–99.

Langley, Ralph H. "The Role of Women in the Church." *Southwestern Journal of Theology* 19/2 (Spring 1977): 60–72.

Lawhon, Sharon Leding. "Women: Leading and Planning Worship." *Baptist History and Heritage* 31/3 (July 1996): 48–58.

Letsinger, Norman H. "The Status of Women in the Southern Baptist Convention in Historical Perspective." *Baptist History and Heritage* 12/1 (January 1977): 37–44.

———. "The Women's Liberation Movement: Implications for Southern Baptists." Th.D. dissertation, Southern Baptist Theological Seminary, 1973.

Lumpkin, William L. "The Role of Women in 18th Century Virginia Baptist Life." *Baptist History and Heritage* 8/3 (July 1973): 158–67.

Magee, Nell. "The Ministry Roles of Women." *Search* 9/2 (Winter 1979): 19–24.

Marshall, Molly T. "Persons." In *A Baptist's Theology*, edited by R. Wayne Stacy, 41–59. Macon GA: Smyth & Helwys, 1999.

———. "Toward an Encompassing Theological Vision for Women in Light of Baptist Tradition." *Folio*. Fall 1986. 1–2.

———. "When Keeping Silent No Longer Will Do: A Theological Agenda for the Contemporary Church." *Review and Expositor* 83/1 (Winter 1986): 27–33.

———. "Women in Ministry." In *Formation for Christian Ministry*, edited by Anne Davis and Wade Rowatt Jr., 123–30. Louisville: Review and Expositor, 1981.

———. "Women in Ministry: A Biblical Theology." *Folio*. Fall 1983. 1.

———. "Women's Status in Ministry Equals That of Men." In *Defining Baptist Convictions: Guidelines for the Twenty-First Century*, edited by Charles W. Deweese, 198–205. Franklin TN: Providence House Publishers, 1996.

Martin, Patricia Summerlin. "Hidden Work: Baptist Women in Texas, 1880–1920." Ph.D. dissertation, Rice University, 1982.

———. "Keeping Silence: Texas Baptist Women's Role in Public Worship, 1800–1920." *Texas Baptist History* 3 (1983): 15–30.

———. "Ordained Work—Unordained Workers, Texas 'Bible Women,' 1800–1920." *Texas Baptist History* 8 (1988): 1–9.

Maston, T. B. "The Bible and Women." *The Student* 64/8 (February 1985): 4–6, 47–48.

McBeth, Leon. "The Changing Role of Women in Baptist History." *Southwestern Journal of Theology* 22/1 (Fall 1979): 84–96.

———. "The Ordination of Women." *Review and Expositor* 78/4 (Fall 1981): 515–30.

———. "Perspectives on Women in Baptist Life." *Baptist History and Heritage* 22/3 (July 1987): 4–11.

———. "The Role of Women in Southern Baptist History." *Baptist History and Heritage* 12/1 (January 1977): 3–25

———. "Women Deacons." In *Encyclopedia of Southern Baptists*, 4:2558. Nashville TN: Broadman Press, 1982.

———. *Women in Baptist Life*. Nashville: Broadman Press, 1979.

———. "Women in Ministry." In *Encyclopedia of Southern Baptists*, 4:2559. Nashville: Broadman Press, 1982.

Miller, Ann. "The Ordination of Women Among Texas Baptists." *Perspectives in Religious Studies* 29/3 (Fall 2002): 269–88.

Miller, Elizabeth J. "AB Women's Gains and Losses Three Decades after the Integration of the Mission Societies." *American Baptist Quarterly* 20/3 (September 2001): 227–37.

Morgan, David T. *Southern Baptist Sisters: In Search of Status, 1845–2000*. Macon GA: Mercer University Press, 2003.

Morrison, Karen Lyn. "Persistence in Honoring Self as Expressed in the Lives of Ordained Southern Baptist Women." Ph.D., dissertation, Texas Women's University, 1995.

Music, David W. "Heroines of Baptist Hymnody." *Baptist History and Heritage* 29/1 (January 1994): 45–53.

Patterson, Dorothy Kelley. "Why I Believe Southern Baptists Churches Should Not Ordain Women." *Baptist History and Heritage* 23/3 (July 1988): 56–62.

Pearce, Betty McGary. "A History of Women in Ministry, SBC." *Folio.* Summer 1985. 9–10.

Price, Clay L. "A Survey of Southern Baptist Attitudes toward Women in Church and Society." Master's thesis, West Georgia College, 1978.

"Report of the American Baptist Churches Task Force on Women." *American Baptist Quarterly* 20/3 (September 2001): 267–69.

Rogers, Joyce. "God's Chief Assignment to Women." *The Southern Baptist Journal* 2/1 (January 1974): 3, 9.

Scales, T. Laine. *"All That Fits a Woman": Training Southern Baptist Women for Charity and Mission, 1907–1926.* Macon GA: Mercer University Press, 2000.

Schaller, Thelma. "American Baptist Women's Contributions to Leadership Development in the Twentieth Century." *American Baptist Quarterly* 20/3 (September 2001): 242–51.

Sehested, Nancy Hasting. "Women and Ministry in the Local Congregation." *Review and Expositor* 83/1 (Winter 1986): 71–79.

Shaw, Susan M. "'Once There Was a Camelot': Women Doctoral Graduates of The Southern Baptist Theological Seminary, 1982–1992, Talk about the Seminary, the Fundamentalist Takeover, and Their Lives Since SBTS." *Review and Expositor* 95/3 (Summer 1998): 397–423.

Shurden, Kay. "The Impact of Southern Baptist Women on Social Issues: Family Issues." *Baptist History and Heritage* 22/3 (July 1987): 33–36.

Sisk, Ron. "Women in the SBC: A Status Report." *The Student* 64/8 (February 1985): 45.

Sorrill, Bobbie. "Southern Baptist Laywomen in Missions." *Baptist History and Heritage* 22/3 (July 1987): 21–28.

Spoolstra, Linda C. "Project S.W.I.M: A Study of Women in Ministry." *American Baptist Quarterly* 20/3 (September 2001): 238–41.

————. "Update on S.W.I.M.—1985." *American Baptist Quarterly* 20/3 (September 2001): 279–83.

Stagg, Evelyn O. "Looking Back In Order to Move Ahead." *Folio*. Spring 1985. 1–2.

Stancil, Bill. "Divergent Views and Practices of Ordination Among Southern Baptists Since 1945." *Baptist History and Heritage* 23/3 (July 1988): 42–49.

Stricklin, David. "Community and Faithfulness: A Genealogy of Dissident Southern Baptist Women." In *A Genealogy of Dissent: Southern Baptist Protest in the Twentieth Century* by David Stricklin, 114–41. Lexington: University of Kentucky Press, 1999.

Sumners, Bill. "Southern Baptist Women and Women's Right to Vote, 1910–1920." *Baptist History and Heritage* 12/1 (January 1977): 45–51.

Sutton, Carol Franklin. "What Do You See?" *American Baptist Quarterly* 20/3 (September 2001): 295–97.

Thompson, Evelyn W. "Southern Baptist Women as Writers and Editors." *Baptist History and Heritage* 22/3 (July 1987): 50–58.

Trull, Joe, and Audra Trull, editors. *Putting Women in Their Place: Moving Beyond Gender Stereotypes in Church and Home*. Macon GA: Smyth & Helwys Publishing, Inc., 2003.

Vickers, Gregory. "Models of Womanhood and the Early Woman's Missionary Union." *Baptist History and Heritage* 24/1 (January 1989): 41–53.

Weatherford, Carolyn. "Shaping of Leadership Among Southern Baptist Women." *Baptist History and Heritage* 23/3 (July 1987): 12–20.

"Women in Ministry." *The Southern Baptist Journal* 15/3 (July–September 1987): 1–7.

Younger, Doris Anne. "American Baptist Women: The Violet Rudd Years, 1951–1976." *American Baptist Quarterly* 20/3 (September 2001): 284–94.

Ziegler, Valarie H. "Genesis and Gender Roles: The Southern Baptist Debate over Women's Ordination." http://iupress.indiana.edu/instruct_guide/eve&adam/debate.html (accessed September 17, 2004).\

# End Notes

---

Chapter One

[1] H. Leon McBeth, "Perspectives on Women in Baptist Life," *Baptist History and Heritage* 22/3 (July 1987): 10.

[2] Alister E. McGrath, *Christian Theology: An Introduction*, 3rd ed. (Oxford: Blackwell Publishers, 2001) 169.

[3] Ibid., 167.

[4] Eugene H. Peterson, *Leap over a Wall: Earthy Spirituality for Everyday Christians* (San Francisco: HarperSanFrancisco, 1997) 3.

[5] Stanley J. Grenz, *Theology for the Community of God* (Grand Rapids MI: William B. Eerdmans Publishing Company, 1994) 6.

[6] Ibid., 425.

[7] Ibid., 425–26.

[8] Alister E. McGrath, *Christian Spirituality* (Oxford: Blackwell Publishers, 1999) 119.

[9] *A Discoverie of Six Women Preachers in Middlesex, Kent, Cambridgeshire and Salisbury* (n.p., 1641). Although the six women are not specifically identified as Baptists, Baptist scholars such as Edward Caryl Starr and William Thomas Whitley include this document in their bibliographies of Baptist writings, indicating that the women were Baptists. See Edward Caryl Starr, *A Baptist Bibliography: Being a Register of Printed Mataerial by and about Baptists, Including Works Written against the Baptists*, 25 vols. (Philadelphia: Judson Press, 1947–1976) and William Thomas Whitley, *A Baptist Bibliography: Being a Register of the Chief Materials for Baptist History, Whether in Manuscript or in Print, Preserved in England, Wales, and Ireland*, 2 vols. (London: Kingsgate Press, 1916–1922). Carolyn Blevins also believes these women to be Baptist. See Carolyn D. Blevins, *Women's Place in Baptist Life*, The Baptist Heritage Library (Brentwood TN: Baptist History and Heritage, 2003) 26. For more on British Baptist women, see Anthony Richard Barker, "Women's Roles in the Baptist Churches: An Historical and

Contemporary Reflection on Baptist Female Leadership in Britain" (Master's thesis, University of Oxford, 1996), http://www.baptist.org.uk/Resources/downloads/ma_tbarker.pdf (accessed January 10, 2005).

[10] *A Discoverie of Six Women Preachers*, 1.

[11] Quoted in Dorothy P. Ludlow, "Shaking Patriarchy's Foundations: Sectarian Women in England, 1641–1700," in *Triumph over Silence: Women in Protestant History*, Contributions to the Study of Religion 15, ed. Richard L. Greaves (Westport CT: Greenwood Press, 1985) 96.

[12] Thomas Edwards, *Gangraena: Or a Catalogue and Discovery of Many of the Errours, Heresies, Blasphemies, and Pernicious Practices of the Sectaries of This Time* (London: Printed for Ralph Smith, 1645) 1:86.

[13] John H. Briggs, "She-Preachers, Widows and Other Women: The Feminine Dimension in Baptist Life Since 1600," *Baptist Quarterly* 31/7 (July 1986): 339–40.

[14] The seven women members were Mary Williams, Mary Sweet Holliman, Catherine Scott, Mary Small Olney, Mrs. Westcott, Mrs. Throckmorton, and Widow Reese. See Henry Melville King, ed., *Historical Catalogue of the Members of the First Baptist Church in Providence, Rhode Island* (Providence: Townsend, F. H., Printer, 1908) 22–23.

[15] John Winthrop, *The Journal of John Winthrop, 1630–1649*, abr. ed., ed. Richard S. Dunn and Laetitia Yeandle (Cambridge MA: The Belknap Press of Harvard University Press, 1996) 155.

[16] James Taylor, *Lives of Virginia Baptist Ministers*, 2nd ed. (Richmond: Yale & Wyatt, 1838) 265–66.

[17] Ibid., 340–43.

[18] Robert Semple, *History of the Rise and Progress of the Baptists in Virginia* (Richmond: privately printed, 1810) 374.

[19] E. Glenn Hinson, *A History of Baptists in Arkansas* (Little Rock: Arkansas Baptist State Convention, 1979) 100.

[20] G. S. Bailey, *A Call to Ministry* (Chicago: Church and Goodman, n.d.) 1.

[21] Dotson M. Nelson Jr., "Minister, The Southern Baptist," in *Encyclopedia of Southern Baptists* (Nashville: Broadman Press, 1958) 2:860.

[22] H. Leon McBeth, *Women in Baptist Life* (Nashville: Broadman Press, 1979) 103–104.

[23] H. Leon McBeth, *The First Baptist Church of Dallas: Centennial History, 1868–1968* (Grand Rapids MI: Zondervan Publishing House, 1968) 66, 131.

[24] H. Richard Niebuhr and Daniel D. Williams, eds., introduction to *The Ministry in Historical Perspectives* (New York: Harper and Brothers, 1956) viii.

[25] Ibid., ix. See also Bill Pitts, "Current Trends in Texas Baptist Ordination," *Perspectives in Religious Studies* 29/3 (Fall 2002): 266.

[26] Bill Stancil, "Divergent Views and Practices of Ordination Among Southern Baptists Since 1945," *Baptist History and Heritage* 23/3 (July 1988): 43.

[27] McBeth, *Women in Baptist Life*, 164.

[28] Stancil, "Divergent Views and Practices of Ordination," 44.

[29] Morris Ashcraft, "Introduction: Called by God: Affirmed by the Church," in *God-Called Ministry: Essays on the Christian Ministry*, ed. Morris Ashcraft(Cary: The Baptist State Convention of North Carolina, n.d.) 17. See also Pitts, "Current Trends in Texas Baptist Ordination," 266.

[30] For a discussion of the biblical basis for ordination, see R. Alan Culpepper, "The Biblical Basis for Ordination," *Review and Expositor* 78/4 (Fall 1981): 471–84, and the following articles in the Summer 2002 (29/2) issue of *Perspectives in Religious Studies*: Thomas Brisco, "Old Testament Antecedents to Ordination," 159–75; Susan M. Pigott, "A Response to 'The Old Testament Antecedents for Ordination' by Thomas Briscoe," 177–82; David E. Garland, "The Absence of an Ordained Ministry in the Churches of Paul," 183–95; Todd D. Still, "Historical Anachronism and Ministerial Ordination: A Response to David E. Garland," 197–203; Sharyn Dowd, "'Ordination' in Acts and the Pastoral Epistles," 205–17; and R. Robert Creech, "A Response to '"Ordination" in Acts and the Pastoral Epistles,'" 219–21.

[31] Frank Stagg, *New Testament Theology* (Nashville: Broadman Press, 1962) 253. See also Ashcraft, "Introduction," 17.

[32] John Knox, "The Ministry in the Primitive Church," in *The Ministry in Historical Perspectives*, ed. H. Richard Niebuhr and Daniel D. Williams (New York: Harper and Brothers, 1956) 1.

[33] Winthrop S. Hudson, *Baptists in Transition: Individualism and Christian Responsibility* (Valley Forge PA: Judson Press, 1979) 53.

[34] As Finley Edge observed, "This means that *the primary responsibility for God's ministry in the world is the responsibility of the laity and not the clergy.*" See Finley B. Edge, *The Greening of the Church* (n.p., 1981) 43.

[35] For example, see Eph. 4:11–12.

[36] Hudson, *Baptists in Transition*, 53.

[37] Ashcraft, "Introduction," 8–9; Fisher Humphreys, "Call and Ordination: Commissioned to Ministry," in *God-Called Ministry: Essays on the Christian Ministry* (Cary: The Baptist State Convention of North Carolina, n.d.) 89.

[38] G. Hugh Wamble, "Baptist Ordination Practices to 1845," *Baptist History and Heritage* 23/3 (July 1988): 16.

[39] Stancil, "Divergent Views and Practices of Ordination," 43.

[40] *The Ordination of Baptist Ministers: A Paper Presented Jointly by the Faculties of the Southern Baptist Theological Seminary, Southwestern Baptist Theological Seminary, and New Orleans Baptist Theological Seminary* (Nashville: Broadman Press, n.d.) 3.

[41] Fisher Humphreys, "Women in Christian Ministry," in *Putting Women in Their Place: Moving beyond Gender Stereotypes in Church and Home*, ed. Joe Trull and Audra Trull (Macon GA: Smyth & Helwys Publishing Inc., 2003) 143.

[42] Stancil, "Divergent Views and Practices of Ordination," 43.

[43] [Charles H. Spurgeon], *The Autobiography of Charles H. Spurgeon, 1834–1854* (Cincinnati: Curts & Jennings) 1:356.

[44] C. H. Spurgeon, "The Holy Spirit Glorifying Christ" (sermon, August 17, 1862), http://www.biblebb.com/files/spurgeon/0465.HTM (accessed January 9, 2005).

[45] Dorothy Kelley Patterson, "Why I Believe Southern Baptist Churches Should Not Ordain Women," *Baptist History and Heritage* 23/3 (July 1988): 59.

[46] For more information about Baptist women's ordination, see Ann Miller, "The Ordination of Women Among Texas Baptists," *Perspectives in Religious Studies* 29/3 (Fall 2002): 269–88; Rosalie Beck, "A Response to 'The Ordination of Women Among Texas Baptists' by Ann Miller," *Perspectives in Religious Studies* 29/3 (Fall 2002): 289–93; and Leon McBeth, "The Ordination of Women," *Review and Expositor* 78/4 (Fall 1981): 515–30.

[47] *Year Book*, American Baptist Convention, 1965–1966, 74.

[48] *Annual*, Southern Baptist Convention, 1984, 65.

[49] *Baptist Faith and Message* (Nashville TN: LifeWay, 2000) 13.

[50] David Hines, interview by Pamela R. Durso, January 12, 2005, notes in interviewer's possession.

[51] Rodney L. Henry and The Committee on Faith and Order, *A Manual of Procedures for Seventh Day Baptist Churches with An Account of Their Basis in Seventh Day Baptist Polity and Beliefs* (Janesville WI: Seventh Day Baptist General Conference of USA and Canada) H-5.

[52] Gordon Lawton, interview by Pamela R. Durso, January 14, 2005, notes in interviewer's possession. Lawton is the Director of Pastoral Services for the Center on Ministry at the Seventh Day Baptist General Conference, USA and Canada, Limited.

[53] J. Matthew Pinson, *A Free Will Baptist Handbook: Heritage, Beliefs, Ministries* (Nashville: Randall House Publications, 1998) 76.

[54] Wayne Camp, "The Sandy Creek Baptist Church (Part 1)" *The Grace Proclamator and Promulgator*, February 1, 2002, http://www.gpp-5grace.com/graceproclamator/pp0202_complete.htm (accessed January 10, 2005).

[55] Bill J. Leonard, *Baptist Ways: A History* (Valley Forge PA: Judson Press, 2003) 280.

[56] Eric Lincoln and Lawrence H. Mamiya, "The Ordination of Women," in *Baptists in the Balance*, ed. Everett C. Goodwin (Valley Forge PA: Judson Press, 1997) 120.

⁵⁷ Stancil, "Divergent Views and Practices of Ordination," 46.

⁵⁸ Humphreys, "Women in Christian Ministry," 143.

⁵⁹ *The Ordination of Baptist Ministers*, 2.

⁶⁰ Marianne Meye Thompson, "Response to Richard Longenecker," in *Women, Authority and the Bible*, ed. Alvera Mickelsen (Downers Grove IL: InterVarsity Press, 1986) 94.

⁶¹ Patricia Gundry, *Neither Slave Nor Free: Helping Women Answer the Call to Church Leadership* (San Francisco: Harper & Row, 1987) vi.

⁶² Ibid., vi-vii.

⁶³ Frederick Buechner, *Wishful Thinking: A Theological ABC* (New York: Harper & Row, Publishers, 1973) 95.


Chapter Two

¹ Cody Lowe, "Pastor says furor over her ordination didn't bother her," *Virginian-Pilot*, September 4, 2004, B10.

² Addie Davis, interview by Eljee Bentley, June 9, 1985, taped interview located in the WMU Archives at the Woman's Missionary Union, SBC, Alma Hunt Library in Birmingham, AL.

³ Ibid.

⁴ Lowe, "Pastor says…," B10.

⁵ Davis, interview by Bentley.

⁶ Ibid.

⁷ Ibid.

⁸ Ibid. Addie does not remember the exact dates of her interim pastorate, only that it was sometime during the 1950s.

⁹ Addie Davis, interview by Pamela R. Durso, December 8, 2004, notes in interviewer's possession.

¹⁰ Davis, interview by Bentley.

¹¹ Ibid.

¹² Ibid.

¹³ Ibid.

¹⁴ Ibid.

[15] "What Ever Happened to Addie Davis?" *Called and Committed*, February 1979, 1; Lowe, "Pastor says...," B10.

[16] Ibid.

[17] George Sheridan, "Tremors of Change," *Home Missions* 43/5, May 1972, 26.

[18] "Reflections on the August 9, 1964 Ordination of Addie Davis: Written Upon the Celebration of the Fortieth Anniversary of this Ordination August 8, 2004" (bulletin, Watts Street Baptist Church, Durham, NC, August 8, 2004).

[19] Ibid.

[20] Ibid. See also Sheridan, "Tremors of Change," 27; and "What Ever Happened to Addie Davis?" 1.

[21] Davis, interview by Bentley.

[22] Ibid.

[23] Lowe, "Pastor says...." B10.

[24] Laura Johnson and John Pierce, "'A Day to Remember': N.C. Church Marks 40th Anniversary of First Female Southern Baptist Minister's Ordination," *Baptists Today*, October 2004, 38.

[25] Addie Davis, "A Dream to Cherish," *Folio*, Autumn 1984, 1.

[26] Davis, interview by Bentley.

[27] Davis, "A Dream to Cherish," 1.

[28] Ibid.

[29] Davis, interview by Bentley; Davis, "A Dream to Cherish," 1; "What Ever Happened to Addie Davis?" 4.

[30] Davis, interview by Bentley.

[31] Ibid.

[32] "What Ever Happened to Addie Davis?" 1.

[33] Davis, interview by Bentley; Lowe, "Pastor says...." B10.

[34] "What Ever Happened to Addie Davis?" 4.

[35] Ibid., 4.

[36] Davis, interview by Bentley.

[37] Ibid.

[38] "What Ever Happened to Addie Davis?" 4.

[39] Davis, "A Dream to Cherish," 8.

[40] Ibid.

[41] Addie Davis, "Four Important Words" (sermon, Watts Street Baptist Church, Durham NC, August 8, 2004). See also Cody Lowe, "Pioneer preacher abides in patience and realism," *Roanoke Times*, Sunday, August 29, 2004, http://www.roanoke.com/columnists/lowe/9912.htm (accessed October 11, 2004). The hymn referred to is "Dear Lord and Father of Mankind."

[42] Davis, interview by Durso.

[43] Lowe, "Pastor says...," B10.

[44] Davis, interview by Bentley.

[45] Ibid.

[46] Davis, "A Dream to Cherish," 1.

[47] Ibid., 8.

[48] Davis, interview by Bentley.


Chapter Six

[1] Mary Brown, "I'll Go Where You Want Me to Go," http://www.cyberhymnal. org/htm/i/g/igowhere.htm (accessed December 8, 2004).

Chapter Seven

[1] T. S. Eliot, *The Complete Poems and Plays 1909–1950* (New York: Harcourt, Brace & World, Inc. 1971) 145.

[2] Margaret Hess, "Women's Ways of Preaching" (D.Min. thesis, Andover Newton Theological School, 1994).

[3] Eliot, *The Complete Poems and Plays*, 145.


Chapter Eight

[1] This article is based on numerous interviews Catherine Allen did with Alma Hunt during the course of writing the history of the Woman's Missionary Union and coauthoring several books with her. Allen also interviewed Hunt in early October 2004.

[2] After her ordination, Aline Fuselier soon found a new home in the Disciples of Christ and has continued as a minister and pastoral counselor in that denomination.

[3] Alice Hunt to Alma Hunt, n.d. The letter is in the possession of Catherine Allen.

[4] Earl Stallings would eventually be unmercifully driven out of town by those who resisted his sense of justice concerning the racial crisis in Birmingham. He was a man ahead of his times in many ways.

Note: Parts of this article are drawn from the Belote Lectures "A New Reformation?: Women in Ministry," which I delivered at the Hong Kong Baptist Theological Seminary, Spring 1999. These lectures were later published in the seminary's journal.

Chapter Nine

[1] W. Morgan Patterson, *Baptist Successionism: A Critical View* (Valley Forge PA: Judson Press, 1969).

[2] See his collection of essays, some of which are largely autobiographical, *Roots of a Radical* (London: SCM Press, 1980).

[3] Molly T. Marshall, "A Brief History and Philosophy of Theological Education at Central Baptist Theological Seminary," *Baptist History and Heritage* 34/3 (Summer/Fall 1999): 21–28.

[4] 1 Tim 2:12.

[5] *A Singing Faith* (Philadelphia: The Westminster Press, 1987) 68.

Chapter Ten

[1] Martha Simmons, "An Interview with Ella Pearson Mitchell," *African American Pulpit* 3/4 (Fall 2000): 91. Some examples of Ella's sermons can be found in Ella Pearson Mitchell, ed., *Those Preaching Women: More Sermons by Black Women Preachers* (Valley Forge PA: Judson Press, 1985) 2:81–87; Ella Pearson Mitchell, ed., *Those Preaching Women: African American Preachers Tackle Tough Questions* (Valley Forge PA: Judson Press, 1996) 3:72–77; David Albert Farmer and Edwina Hunter, eds., *And Blessed Is She: Sermons by Women* (Valley Forge PA: Judson Press, 1994) 203–10; and Jacqueline B.

Glass, ed., *Fire in the Well: Sermons by Ella and Henry Mitchell* (Valley Forge PA: Judson Press, 2003) 3–40. See also Ella Pearson Mitchell, "Rejoice Always," *African American Pulpit* 1/2 (Spring 1998): 25–31; Ella Pearson Mitchell, "All Flesh," *African American Pulpit* 2/2 (Spring 1999): 50–56; and Ella Pearson Mitchell, "Redigging the Wells," *African American Pulpit* 2/4 (Fall 1999): 40–46.

[2] Samuel K. Roberts, ed., introduction to *Born to Preach: Essays in Honor of the Ministry of Henry & Ella Mitchell* (Valley Forge PA: Judson Press, 2000) viii.

[3] Patricia A. Gould-Champ, "Women and Preaching: Telling the Story in Our Own Voice," in *Born to Preach: Essays in Honor of the Ministry of Henry & Ella Mitchell* (Valley Forge PA: Judson Press, 2000) 111.

[4] Gardner C. Taylor, forward to *Fire in the Well: Sermons by Ella and Henry Mitchell*, ed. Jacqueline B. Glass (Valley Forge PA: Judson Press, 2003) ix.

[5] Ella P. Mitchell, "In the Same Year That Mama Died, I Also Saw the Lord," in *The Irresistible Urge to Preach: A Collection of African American "Call" Stories*, The McCreary Center Series in Black Church Studies 1, by William H. Myers (Atlanta: Aaron Press, 1992) 259.

[6] "A Conversation with Ella Pearson Mitchell," *Union News*, Fall 1993, 2.

[7] Mitchell, "In the Same Year," 259.

[8] Simmons, "An Interview with Ella Pearson Mitchell," 91. See also Mitchell, "In the Same Year," 259.

[9] "A Conversation with Ella Pearson Mitchell," 2; Mitchell, "In the Same Year," 259.

[10] Mitchell, "In the Same Year," 260. See also Ella Pearson Mitchell, "Whom God Chooses, God Uses," in *Fire in the Well*, ed. Jacqueline B. Glass (Valley Forge PA: Judson Press, 2003) 39.

[11] "A Conversation with Ella Pearson Mitchell," 2; Mitchell, "In the Same Year," 261.

[12] Simmons, "An Interview with Ella Pearson Mitchell," 93.

[13] Mitchell, "In the Same Year," 260.

[14] "A Conversation with Ella Pearson Mitchell," 2. Ella earned her Doctor of Ministry degree in 1974 from the Claremont School of Theology. In 1989, the fiftieth anniversary of her college graduation, Talladega College honored her with an LHD (Honorary Doctor of Humane Letters).

[15] Mitchell, "In the Same Year," 261–62.

[16] Ibid., 262.

[17] Ibid., 261.

[18] Marvin A. McMickle, "Mitchell, Ella Pearson," in *An Encyclopedia of African American Christian Heritage*, by Marvin A. McMickle (Valley Forge PA: Judson Press, 2002) 74. For examples of their dialogue sermons, see Glass, ed., *Fire in the Well*, 101–57, and Ella Pearson Mitchell and Henry H. Mitchell, "Horseless Carriages That Fly," *African American Pulpit* 1/4 (Fall 1998): 38–43. The Mitchells have also written together. See their "Women: A Historical Perspective," in *Women: To Preach or Not to Preach—21 Outstanding Black Preachers Say Yes!*, ed. Ella Pearson Mitchell (Valley Forge PA: Judson Press, 1991) 1–17, and their *Together for Good: Lessons from Fifty-Five Years of Marriage* (Kansas City MO: Andrews McMeel Publishers, 1999). For a dialogue sermon by Ella and her daughter, see Ella Pearson Mitchell and Elizabeth Mitchell Clement, "Healing for the Household," *African American Pulpit* 3/2 (Spring 2000): 99–104.

[19] Roberts, introduction to *Born to Preach*, vii.

[20] Mitchell, "In the Same Year," 261.

[21] Mitchell, "Whom God Chooses, God Uses," 39.

[22] Mitchell, "In the Same Year," 262.

[23] Ella Pearson Mitchell, "Introduction: Women in the Ministry," in *Those Preachin' Women: Sermons by Black Women Preachers*, ed. Ella Pearson Mitchell (Valley Forge PA: Judson Press, 1985) 1:14.

[24] Ella Pearson Mitchell, "Women in the Pulpit, African American," in *Encyclopedia of African American Religions*, ed. Larry G. Murphy, J. Gordon Melton, and Gary L. Ward (New York: Garland Publishing, 1993) 847.

[25] Ella Mitchell, "The Stumbling Enemy," in *And Blessed Is She: Sermons by Women*, ed. David Albert Farmer and Edwina Hunter (Valley Forge PA: Judson Press, 1994) 209.

[26] Mitchell, "Women in the Pulpit, African American," 851.

[27] Mitchell, "In the Same Year That," 261.

[28] "A Conversation with Ella Pearson Mitchell," 2. See also Simmons, "An Interview with Ella Pearson Mitchell," 93.

[29] Mitchell, "Introduction: Women in the Ministry," 13; Simmons, "An Interview with Ella Pearson Mitchell," 93.

[30] Mitchell, "Introduction: Women in the Ministry," 19–20.

[31] Simmons, "An Interview with Ella Pearson Mitchell," 93.

[32] Mitchell, "Introduction: Women in the Ministry," 19.

[33] Mitchell, introduction to *Those Preaching Women*, 2:15.

[34] Simmons, "An Interview with Ella Pearson Mitchell," 93–94.

[35] Mitchell, introduction to *Those Preaching Women*, 2:14.

[36] Ibid., 2:14–15.

[37] Simmons, "An Interview with Ella Pearson Mitchell," 93.

[38] Mitchell, "The Stumbling Enemy," 209.

[39] Acts 2:17; Mitchell, "Introduction: Women in the Ministry," 11.

[40] Ibid., 13–14.

[41] Ibid. 14. Mitchell deals with the problem passages on 17–18. See also Mitchell, introduction to *Those Preaching Women*, 2:14, and her Hampton Minister's Conference lecture, "A Woman's Word from the Lord, *African American Pulpit* 5/2 (Spring 2002): 38–42. Ella and her husband, Henry, discuss the status of women in the Bible and in church history in Ella Pearson Mitchell and Henry H. Mitchell, "Women: A Historical Perspective," in *Women: To Preach or Not to Preach*, 1–17.

[42] See the following scriptures for references to these women: Deborah (Jdgs 4:4–8), Huldah (2 Kgs 22:12–20; 2 Chr 34:19–28), Pricilla (Acts 18:24), the women prophets at Corinth (1 Cor 11:5), and Philip's daughters (Acts 21:8–9).

[43] Mitchell, "Introduction: Women in the Ministry," 12.

[44] Mitchell, "Whom God Chooses, God Uses," 39.

[45] Joel 2:28–29

[46] Mitchell, "Introduction: Women in the Ministry," 19.

[47] Mitchell, "Whom God Chooses, God Uses," 40.

[48] Simmons, "An Interview with Ella Pearson Mitchell," 93–94.

[49] Ibid., 93–94.

[50] Ibid., 93.

[51] Ibid., 93.

[52] Ibid., 94.

[53] Simmons, "An Interview with Ella Pearson Mitchell," 94.

[54] Mitchell, "Women in the Pulpit, African American," 851.

[55] Simmons, "An Interview with Ella Pearson Mitchell," 94.

[56] Ibid., 94.

[57] Mitchell, "Women in the Pulpit, African American," 851–52.

[58] McMickle, "Mitchell, Ella Pearson," 73.

[59] Gould-Champ, "Women and Preaching: Telling the Story in Our Own Voice," in *Born to Preach*, 110–11.

[60] Program insert, 1994 Distinguished Alumi/ae Award Service, Virginia Union University School of Theology, May 6, 1994. Ella has served God in numerous positions in her life, among which are the following: Sunday School Missionary (South Carolina); Minister of Education at the Church of the Master (New York City); Minister of Education at Second Baptist Church (Los Angeles); Associate Professor of Christian Education at Proctor School of Theology at Virginia Union University; Adjunct Professor of Christian Education at the American Baptist Seminary of the West and at Laverne University; and first female Dean of Sisters Chapel at Spelman College (Atlanta). Ella also taught at the American Baptist Seminary of the West; Claremont School of Theology; La Verne University; Compton College; Santa Monica City College; and the public schools of Fresno and Claremont, all in California. Ella also held a joint appointment with her husband as Visiting Professors of Homiletics at the Interdenominational Theological Center (Atlanta).

Chapter Eleven

[1] This article was adapted from a feature story, titled "When God Called 'Miss Ruby,'" which appeared in the May 2003 issue of *Baptists Today*.